The American Secretary of State

AN INTERPRETATION

The American Secretary of State

AN INTERPRETATION

Alexander DeConde

PALL MALL PRESS
LONDON AND DUNMOW

FIRST PUBLISHED 1962 BY FREDERICK A. PRAEGER, INC.
NEW YORK

PUBLISHED IN GREAT BRITAIN 1963 BY
PALL MALL PRESS LTD.

2 CLEMENT'S INN, LONDON WC2, AND DUNMOW, ESSEX

PRINTED IN THE UNITED STATES OF AMERICA

FOR JEANNE

A PRAYER ON BECOMING SECRETARY OF STATE

O God, my only trust was thou
     Through all life's scenes before:
Lo, at thy throne again I bow,
     New mercies to implore.

Thy aid, O Father, wilt thou lend?
     My thoughts wilt thou inspire?
My heart to do thy pleasure bend?
     My breast to virtue fire?

Thy gracious wisdom to fulfill
     My constant aim incline,
Grant for my feeble, faltering will
     Th' unerring strength of thine.

Grant active powers, grant fervid zeal,
     And guide by thy control,
And ever be my country's weal
     The purpose of my soul.

Thine be the purpose, thine the deed,
     Which thou alone canst bless.
From thee all perfect gifts proceed,
     Oh, crown them with success.

Extend, all-seeing God, thy hand,
     In mercy still decree,
And make to bless my native land
     An instrument of me.

JOHN QUINCY ADAMS
(*Written when he assumed
his duties as Secretary of
State, September 21, 1817*)

Preface

Iɴ 1957, Dwight D. Eisenhower told newspapermen that the position of Secretary of State is "the greatest and most important job in the world." Although the President's statement was a deliberate exaggeration intended to stress his unflagging support of John Foster Dulles, then under attack in Congress and elsewhere, it was no more than accurate in recognizing that the shadow of the Secretaryship has become so big that it stretches around the earth. The Secretary appears to mankind a symbol of America, the official spokesman of the American Government on matters of foreign policy. His words and deeds have worldwide repercussions.

Despite the growth in importance of the Secretaryship of State, no one person, to my knowledge, has ever written a historical analysis of that office. Few, moreover, seem to have a solid understanding of the Secretary's role in the making of foreign policy. This study offers an interpretation of the Secretaryship—in effect, a brief biography of the office. It is more an introduction than a monograph and hence makes no claim to comprehensiveness. It concentrates primarily on the Secretary's power, his personal influence in the conduct of foreign relations and the influence he and his office have had and do have in government. It attempts to explain some of the Secretary's history and responsibilities and, most of all, his relationship to the President. This book does not deal with the details of the Secretary's diplomacy, his administrative functions, or his relations with other agencies in the government. Those aspects of the Secretaryship may be found elsewhere. I have tried in my analysis to combine the techniques of the historian and the political scientist, and in doing so, I have examined principles that may give some understanding of the Secretaryship as a historical institution.

My main theme is the conventional one that the power of the Secretary of State depends on his relations with the President and hence is personal more than institutional. I cannot accept the platitude that "every President must be his own Secretary of State"; power in the Secretaryship, in the sense that the Secretary participates in the making of high-level decisions, is flexible. Whether that flexibility derives from the Presidency alone or is intrinsic in the Secretaryship itself, it is clear that the Secretary of State often stands next to the summit of power in the American system of government. This analysis tries to show why this has been and is so.

A number of friends and colleagues, in history, political science, psychology, and in the Department of State, have helped me in clarifying my ideas and avoiding errors of fact and interpretation in the writing of this book. It is a pleasure to express publicly my deep gratitude to John R. Alden, John W. Atkinson, Thomas A. Bailey, David D. Burks, Mary P. Chapman, Richard N. Current, Donald F. Drummond, Russell H. Fifield, Sidney Fine, Hugh M. Hall, Harold K. Jacobson, John Tate Lanning, William L. Neumann, E. Taylor Parks, Marvin Zahniser, and Burton F. Beers, who shared some of his research on Robert Lansing with me. Since several of these gracious critics, who have read the manuscript at some stage of its development, disagree with some of the views I express, I must stress that all interpretations are my own. Remaining errors, of course, are mine too. I am indebted to the Horace H. Rackham School of Graduate Studies, of the University of Michigan, for a generous grant from its Faculty Research Fund that has aided me in my research and writing. Lastly, I wish also to point out that some of my time as a Guggenheim Fellow in 1960 was spent in condensing and revising this study for publication.

ALEXANDER DECONDE

Santa Barbara, California

Contents

	Preface	vii
1	Origins and Precedents	1
2	Responsibilities, Powers, Limitations	17
3	Qualifications and Selection	39
4	Heir Apparent and Prime Minister	65
5	The Figurehead	87
6	The Partnership	112
7	Statesmanship and Politics	132
8	The Administrator and Diplomat	154
	Bibliographical Note	175
	Index	179

I

Origins and Precedents

The Congress have wisely put their finances into the
hands of one intelligent person. I wish they would do
the same with their correspondence, by appointing a
single secretary for foreign affairs,
                              —BENJAMIN FRANKLIN, 1781

W HAT may be called the beginnings of the Secretaryship of
State were haphazard. Its domestic functions originated in
the work of Charles Thomson, a fiery patriot of Irish birth known
as "the Sam Adams of Philadelphia," who served as the Secretary
of the Continental Congress throughout its life, that is, from
1774 to 1789. He promulgated the laws and ordinances of Congress, was the keeper of the Great Seal, the official mark of the
nation's sovereignty, and served as the medium of communication between Congress and those affected by its acts. He was, in
effect, a secretary for affairs of state, an administrator without
power in the making of vital decisions.

No one individual at first held responsibility for the more
important matters of foreign affairs. Congress itself controlled
them but placed their operations in the hands of special committees. In November, 1775, more than six months before the
thirteen American colonies made their final break with Great
Britain, the second Continental Congress created the most important of those committees, the Committee of Secret Correspondence, to communicate with friends in Britain, Ireland, and other
parts of the world. Since this standing committee of five was

restricted only by the requirement that it had to place its correspondence before Congress when so directed, it theoretically could act on its own initiative. Its first chairman, Benjamin Franklin, carried the burden of its correspondence and of most of its other work. He may, therefore, be considered America's first executive official directly responsible for foreign affairs, a kind of embryonic secretary of state.

Franklin's committee held secret meetings with a French agent in December, 1775, to discuss possible aid to the rebelling Colonies, and Franklin himself wrote the instructions for America's first diplomatic agent, who went to France as a representative of the committee to seek an alliance. Yet neither Franklin nor the committee was able to gain any real power over foreign relations. Congress, either through other special committees or its committee of the whole, exercised a close control over foreign policy, even over minute administrative details.

In this condition of virtual impotence, with no permanent chairman, divided views, and a fluctuating membership, the Committee of Secret Correspondence survived until April, 1777, when, in keeping with the nation's proclaimed independence, Congress changed the group's name to the "Committee for Foreign Affairs" and appointed Thomas Paine its first secretary. As an organ for the conduct of foreign relations, the new committee proved as ineffective as its predecessor, for Congress would not augment its power along with the change of title.

Paine had hoped to become more than a mere clerk and even considered himself a kind of foreign minister. He frequently arrogated to himself the title "Secretary for Foreign Affairs," but his authority never matched his grandiose idea. As secretary, the pugnacious Paine lasted less than two years, being compelled to resign in January, 1779, for making public, in a quarrel within Congress, information his oath of office had pledged him to keep secret. During the controversy, Gouverneur Morris, a haughty conservative, stressed that Paine served solely at the pleasure of Congress.

James Lovell, a Boston schoolmaster and politician, next be-

came the committee's guiding but faltering spirit. He monoto-
nously complained of his difficulties—neglect by Congress, the
obstacles to squeezing work from a committee whose members
had other pressing obligations, and an inadequate staff. For
months at a time, he himself was the committee, carrying on its
affairs by what he called long hours of "quill-driving" at night
after he had spent a full day in Congress. In one of his complaints, he admitted that "there is really no Such Thing as a
Committee of foreign affairs existing, no Secretary or Clerk, further than I persevere to be one and the other."

Weary of Lovell's excuses for not maintaining correspondence, Benjamin Franklin, then the American Minister in Paris,
sent him a piercing criticism of the committee system in the
handling of foreign affairs, in which he said that they "would
best be managed by one Secretary, who could write when he had
an Opportunity, without waiting for the Concurrence or Opinions of his Brethren, who cannot always be got conveniently
together."

John Jay, at the time on a special diplomatic mission in
Madrid, was equally critical. "One good private correspondent,"
he wrote, "would be worth twenty standing committees, made of
the wisest heads in America, for the purpose of intelligence."

Although in part responsible for Lovell's difficulties, Congress,
too, had become dissatisfied with his work and the chaos in the
management of foreign relations. Even before Franklin and Jay
had expressed their criticisms, others had recognized that the
committee system was failing and that a department of foreign
affairs, headed by a responsible and respected minister, was
needed. Alexander Hamilton, one of the most vigorous of the
critics, wrote that "there is always more decision, more dispatch,
more responsibility, where single men than where bodies are
concerned."

The Articles of Confederation and Perpetual Union, the nation's first constitution, had not made provision for an office
such as the critics desired. Yet the Articles stated that Congress
could appoint such "committees and civil officers as may be

necessary for managing the general affairs of the United States"
—a power capable of broad interpretation. Congress, moreover,
began to consider a reform before the states had ratified the
Articles. In January, 1779, it instructed the Committee for
Foreign Affairs to secure information on how foreign governments managed their executive departments.

Up to this time, the system used in the conduct of foreign
relations had not followed foreign models. It had sprung by
chance, as the need arose, from American roots. Hamilton and
others who had studied the ministries in European governments
had apparently been most impressed by those in France and
England. The principle of control of an executive department
by one man had advanced further in France than in England,
and the example most often used to illustrate the advantage of
centralized control was the work of the Duc de Sully, Henry IV's
powerful minister.

Sometime in 1779, the Committee for Foreign Affairs obtained the information Congress had requested, but Congress
did not act on it until May, 1780, when it appointed a special
committee to consider a proper arrangement for a department of
foreign affairs. The committee submitted a report in June, but
Congress delayed consideration of it until December, when
increased pressure in foreign relations made action imperative.

In its original report, the special committee had urged the
grant of substantial powers to a minister of foreign affairs—
probably patterned after the French model—who could formulate foreign policy. It pointed out that "the most effectual mode
of conducting the business of the Department of Foreign Affairs
would be through a minister vested with confidential powers
after the example of other nations, responsible for his trust and
under the immediate direction of Congress." Jealous of its own
authority over foreign relations and unwilling to surrender any
of it, Congress vetoed the suggestion.

The committee's plan, as modified and finally adopted by
Congress on January 10, 1781, created the Department of Foreign Affairs headed by a Secretary for Foreign Affairs. The new

office was neither that of a mere Congressional clerk nor that of a responsible policy-making minister. It fell somewhere between the two. The new Secretary was to be essentially a high-level administrative officer; he was to be elected by Congress, hold office at its pleasure, serve under its immediate control and supervision, and be responsible to it for his actions. His chief functions were to correspond with the American ministers abroad and to receive the communications of the ministers of foreign powers in the United States. To enable him to explain his reports and to keep informed of domestic developments, he was given the privilege of attending Congress, a privilege that might enable him to take part in the deliberations on foreign policy.

Divided by factional and sectional rivalry, Congress delayed seven months before filling the new post. In August, 1781, it finally elected Robert R. Livingston, lawyer, politician, and Chancellor of the state of New York, as the first Secretary for Foreign Affairs—a choice stemming allegedly from French influence in Congress.

Arthur Lee, the defeated candidate for the Secretaryship, was bitter. "Whatever you see or receive from him you may consider as dictated by the French Minister," Lee said of Livingston. "He made him what he is, and policy, or gratitude, keeps him from disobeying or renouncing his maker."

Having served as a member of the earlier Committee for Foreign Affairs, Livingston fortunately had had some experience with the demands of the new office. Nonetheless, he confessed that he felt unequal to the task, saying the subject was "new to me & foreign to the line in which my studies have lain."

Before accepting the post, Livingston asked for an explanation of its powers, particularly whether he would be given authority to appoint his own subordinates. The president of Congress assured him that his office was "one of the most honorable in the gift of Congress," and that "the liberty to attend Congress, and the constant intercourse with the Members, distinguish it from any other." In September, after Congress had satisfied his inquiry, Livingston accepted.

After three months, Livingston discovered flaws in the obligations and powers of his office and recommended changes. Since Congress was sovereign, he pointed out, an intimate knowledge of its sentiments was necessary if he were properly to carry out his duties, but he could not obtain that knowledge through its public acts or merely by attending its sessions and explaining his reports. In monarchical governments, he said, the minister of foreign affairs is "considered as the most confidential servant of the crown. In republics it is much more difficult to execute this task, as the sentiments of the sovereign sometimes change with the members who compose the sovereignty." He therefore requested the specific right to ask questions and explain his own views when his reports were being debated in Congress. He also asked for the power to act on his own in minor matters, and for more clerical help.

After examining the Secretaryship for Foreign Affairs, a special Congressional committee reported favorably on Livingston's suggestions. Among its recommendations, it urged that the Secretary be assigned a seat that would place him "officially in Congress" and allow him to initiate discussion and defend his policies. This last might have established the precedent for a responsible and politically powerful minister of foreign affairs, but Congress, unwilling to go that far, denied Livingston's basic request. Most of the committee's recommendations were embodied in a law of February 22, 1782, that repealed the act of the previous year establishing the office.

Although the new law made no basic changes, in some instances it enlarged the Secretary's powers and in others defined them more closely than before. He was obliged, for example, to submit correspondence concerning treaties or "other great national subjects" to Congress before sending it. Since the law entrusted him with correspondence on foreign affairs between Congress and the governors of the states, it in effect added a domestic responsibility to his duties. It also changed his title to the "Secretary to the United States of America for the Department of Foreign Affairs."

Despite the reform, the Secretary still found himself narrowly restricted. He had no power of independent action, and even in small matters of administration, Congress was to take the initiative and make the basic decisions. At times, it ignored him and corresponded directly with ministers abroad and with foreign diplomats in Philadelphia, the capital. It also gave special committees power over foreign relations, and those committees, too, often bypassed Livingston.

By disregarding the Secretary and taking the details of foreign policy into its own hands, Congress made his office little more than an administrative bureau. Except for employing his personal influence with Congress, Livingston could do little to shape the nation's foreign policy. The tenure of the first Secretary for Foreign Affairs thus set a precedent in that he suffered disabilities that were to plague some of the later Secretaries of State, particularly those serving under strong Presidents.

In November, 1782, Congress passed a motion, introduced by James Madison, to enlarge the Secretary's power by allowing him greater freedom in correspondence and in the selection of the information he was required to submit to it. Nevertheless, the next month Livingston offered his resignation, giving as his reasons the increase in his duties as Chancellor of New York, a post he had never given up, and a salary inadequate to maintain the dignity of his office. Madison and others suspected that the treatment Livingston had suffered under Congress had induced his resignation. Livingston left the department in June, 1783. Although hampered by severe limitations, he had tried to formulate as well as carry out policy. Even though he was unsuccessful in policy matters, he was a first-class administrator and brought organization to his department and stature to his new office.

Since Congress was still ridden by faction and some members had long been critical of Livingston, few seem to have lamented his departure. One critic wrote that "his Office was misterious, & secret to all those, who ought to have a perfect Knowledge of all it contain'd— It was undoubtedly public to all those, to whom it ought to have been a profound Secret."

Although a number of prominent men sought the office, which attested to its intrinsic importance, members of Congress appeared to prefer no Secretary for Foreign Affairs to one who might come from an opposing faction. They did not, therefore, immediately elect a successor to Livingston, and the duties of his office fell to the first Under Secretary, who soon resigned because Congress would give him no authority to act. The President of Congress then handled the routine matters and Congress itself managed foreign policy through special committees it appointed as specific needs arose. For a year, including the critical period when peace negotiations were being concluded with Great Britain in Paris, the nation had no officer directly responsible for foreign relations.

I.

Congress had for some time been receiving reports of the conspicuous skill John Jay had displayed in the peace negotiations in Paris. In May, 1784, it elected him the second Secretary to the United States of America for the Department of Foreign Affairs. Jay did not learn of his appointment until friends told him on his arrival home from Paris. Although only thirty-nine years old, he had acquired such broad experience that he was eminently qualified to endow the management of foreign relations with a prestige it had long been lacking. He had been President of the Continental Congress, an original member of the Committee of Secret Correspondence, and a key negotiator in the commission that secured England's recognition of American independence. Certainly, he appeared prepared for all aspects of his new post— political, diplomatic, and administrative.

In notifying Jay officially of the appointment, Charles Thomson stressed that "your country stands in need of your abilities in that office. I feel sensibly that it is not only time but highly necessary for us to think and act like a sovereign as well as a free people." The opportunities offered by the office, he said, "will I trust, greatly contribute to raise and promote this Spirit."

Despite this flattery, Jay deferred his decision, notifying Thomson that he would accept only if Congress would establish itself in one place and if he could appoint his own clerks. Congress met those conditions, and Jay assumed his new duties in December.

Interpreting his position as one of influence and authority, Jay was dissatisfied by the vagueness of the powers of his revived office. He believed that the Secretary should actually conduct foreign relations and have a voice in formulating policy. In January, 1785, he sought to clarify his status. "I have some reason, Sir," he told the President of Congress, "to apprehend that I have come into the office of Secretary for foreign affairs with Ideas of its Duties & Rights somewhat different from those which seem to be entertained by Congress."

To meet some of Jay's objections, Congress attempted a clearer definition of his responsibilities. In the following month, it resolved that all communications concerning foreign affairs should be made through the Secretary for the Department of Foreign Affairs. Congress thus conceded what it had previously been reluctant to do. By centralizing foreign relations in Jay's office, it had taken an important step toward making the Secretaryship a truly important organ of government, a step approved by those who wished to endow the office with stability and authority. "If the Office of Foreign Affairs be a proper one, & properly filled," James Madison wrote shortly after, referring to Jay's views, "a reference of all foreign despatches to it in the first instance, is so obvious a course, that any other disposition of them by Congress seems to condemn their own establishment, to affront the Minister in office," and to impair his usefulness in dealing with foreign governments.

Within the limitations of its power, Jay made the most of his office, trying to become a foreign secretary in fact as well as in name. Unlike his predecessor, he took full advantage of his privilege of attending Congress. He decided what papers should or should not be transmitted to it, brought before it any question of foreign affairs he thought necessary, frequently made recommendations as to what course it should follow in foreign policy, and did not hesitate to defend his own policies. In deference to his experience in foreign affairs, Congress listened to him with respect and usually followed his advice.

To outsiders, Jay's influence appeared great. The French consul in New York believed that the Secretary had acquired a "peculiar ascendancy over the members of Congress" and feared that since considerable important business passed through his office, they would "insensibly become accustomed to seeing only through the eyes of Mr. Jay." Two weeks later, he reported that "the political importance of Mr. Jay increases daily," and added, "Congress seems to me to be guided only by his directions, and it is as difficult to obtain anything without the cooperation of that minister as to bring about the rejection of a measure proposed by him."

Even though Congress did not, in fact, always guide itself by its Secretary's advice and suspiciously guarded its authority in foreign relations, it did release more of that authority to Jay than it had previously to any individual. In March, 1785, Jay had reported the form of a commission for John Adams as Minister to England. Although that important work had always been one of the Secretary's functions, it had usually been performed by special committees. This was the first instance in which Congress entrusted the Secretary with it. In July, Congress invested Jay with authority to make and sign a treaty with Don Diego de Gardoqui, an envoy from Spain. This was the first recognition of the Secretary as a negotiator of treaties, a task that had previously been assigned to special commissions. At the same time, Congress appointed a committee to receive communications from the Secretary, another recognition of the growing importance of his office.

In giving Jay the power of negotiator, Congress had stipulated that he would have to submit all propositions, his own and Gardoqui's, to it before acting on any of them. Irked by that restriction, he told Congress in August that "It is proper and common to instruct Ministers on the great Points to be agitated, and to inform them how far they are to insist on some, and how far they may yield on others— But I am inclined to think it is very seldom thought necessary to leave nothing at all to their Discretion." In such a case, he added, "the man ought not to be employed." Several days later, Congress rescinded its galling restriction, insisting only that he could conclude no treaty until it had been submitted to Congress for approval.

Nothing concrete came of the talks with Gardoqui, but Jay's determined efforts in those negotiations to take foreign policy into his own hands alarmed some members of Congress, particularly those from the South. They distrusted his independence and appetite for power, correctly fearing that he would, if he could, have bartered away the right to navigate the Mississippi River to its mouth in return for Spanish commercial concessions beneficial to the Northeast.

In the Gardoqui negotiations, as at other times, Jay suffered under the frustrating supervision of Congress. He believed that his office did not possess the power it should have or he himself deserved. Even though he was able to wield considerable political influence, he could not bring it into full effect because he could seldom swing the great majority of the legislative body to his views. In the case of the Algerian pirates who preyed on American commerce in the Mediterranean, for example, he preferred war to the payment of tribute, but in this instance, as in others, Congress refused to follow his advice.

Jay's experience as Secretary for Foreign Affairs contributed to his conviction that the Congress under the Articles of Confederation was a weak instrument and that the nation needed a stronger and more centralized government, especially for the guidance of its foreign policy. In collaborating with Alexander Hamilton and James Madison to produce the essays of *The Federalist*, in which Jay discussed the need for effective leadership in foreign relations, he lent his pen and the prestige of his office to those men who were bent on replacing the Confederation government.

Although Jay was clearly the servant of Congress, he had striven to become a responsible foreign secretary such as he had

seen in his diplomatic work abroad, and he had partially succeeded. He had won greater power from Congress than had his
predecessor. Under him the Secretaryship, despite its limitations,
had become the foremost executive office of the Confederation
government—a post of prominence and prestige. He had established precedents that were to make its successor, the Secretaryship of State, the highest nonelective office in the land.

II.

Drawing upon the experience of the Confederation era, the
founding fathers at the Constitutional Convention in Philadelphia, in 1787, considered several proposals that would have
surrounded the President with some kind of advisory council
that included a secretary for foreign affairs. Yet the Constitution
they framed provided for such a secretaryship only by implication. It stipulated that the President could require written
opinions from the heads of the executive departments upon any
subject relating to the duties of their offices. It was left to the
first Congress of the new Federal Government, therefore, to
establish an executive office for the management of foreign affairs.

In May, 1789, a month after Congress had assembled, it took
up the question of creating and organizing executive departments. After considerable discussion, James Madison introduced
a motion in the House of Representatives calling for the establishment of departments of foreign affairs, treasury, and war, each
to be headed by a secretary appointed by the President with the
advice and consent of the Senate and subject to removal by the
President.

Objection immediately arose to placing the department of
foreign affairs first and thus ranking its secretary ahead of the
other executive officers. One member of Congress maintained
that the treasury department was the most important and should
be established first. On the basis of experience in the Confederation era, those who favored a strong government argued that the
management of foreign affairs needed buttressing; they insisted

that if there had been a sturdy department of foreign affairs during the Revolution, a great deal of trouble might have been avoided and the war shortened.

The most heated debate centered on whether the power of removal of a department head should be vested in the President alone or should be shared by him and the Senate. Madison saw danger in a dual control of the removal power, contending that the head of a department should be responsible to the President alone and, under that relationship, should have the highest degree of responsibility in the conduct of his office. "Now," he added, "if the heads of the Executive departments are subjected to removal by the President alone, we have in him security for the good behavior of the officer. If he does not conform to the judgment of the President in doing the executive duties of his office, he can be displaced. This makes him responsible to the great Executive power, and makes the President responsible to the public for the conduct of the person he nominated and appointed to aid him in the administration of his department."

If the President could not remove a Secretary without the Senate's consent, then the Senate would, in effect, share the President's responsibility for the Secretary's conduct. This, Madison said, "would abolish at once that great principle of unity and responsibility in the Executive department." In a dual control over the removal of executive officers, moreover, the people could not hold the Senate to any accountability.

Many Congressmen feared the surrender of too much authority to the President, particularly allowing him almost absolute power over his department heads. Such power, they held, would "make the President a monarch." Whether this faction believed that an executive officer, such as the secretary for foreign affairs, should be accountable by something similar to parliamentary responsibility is not clear. They were convinced, apparently, that the department heads had independent constitutional status and hence were not completely dependent on the President.

Madison's ideas prevailed. The House passed his motion and instructed a committee of eleven to prepare bills that would establish the three executive departments. In drawing up the bill for a department of foreign affairs, the committee used the laws of 1781 and 1782 as models. In fact, with some modification, it revived the department and secretarial office that had existed under the Confederation government.

In June, the committee reported bills for a war department and a department of foreign affairs. To give precedence to the department of foreign affairs, Congress considered its bill first. At once the debate on the removal power burst out again. One Congressman stressed that the head of that department "is as much an instrument in the hands of the President, as the pen is the instrument of the Secretary in corresponding with foreign courts. If, then, the Secretary of Foreign Affairs is the mere instrument of the President, one would suppose, on the principle of expediency, this officer should be dependent upon him." Nonetheless, the House struck out the clause explicitly making the proposed Secretary for the Department of Foreign Affairs removable by the President.

As passed by the House and Senate, and signed into law by President George Washington on July 27, 1789, the act created the Department of Foreign Affairs headed by the Secretary for the Department of Foreign Affairs, who was to perform such duties as the President entrusted to him. The few responsibilities it specified were those normally connected with the management of foreign relations. Moreover, the Secretary was to conduct the business of his department "in such manner as the President of the United States shall, from time to time, order or instruct."

The new Secretary was thus given responsibilities similar to those of his immediate predecessor under the Confederation, but instead of holding office at the pleasure of Congress, he did so at the pleasure of the President, for the basic law implied that the President had the exclusive power of removal; he did not need the consent of the Senate before acting. Since the Senate accepted this implication, the debate over the law creating the first of the executive departments resulted in an enhancement of the President's power and in making the Secretary for the

Department of Foreign Affairs his complete subordinate. Although Congress was later to challenge the President's power of removal, that power has always remained exclusively with the President and is one of the means by which he retains mastery over the machinery of foreign policy.

Although the power to remove all three of the original department heads had been vested in the President, all three were not equally subordinate to him. The law establishing the Treasury Department, for instance, did not mention the Secretary of the Treasury's dependence on the President in the conduct of his office. It also assigned that Secretary enumerated duties, whereas the law creating the office of the Secretary for the Department of Foreign Affairs indicated only the general scope of his duties. The Secretary of the Treasury, although dependent on the President for his appointment and tenure, was closer to Congress than was the Secretary for the Department of Foreign Affairs; the Treasury head was subject to the call of Congress, was more closely hemmed in by statutes, and had a greater freedom of action under the President.

To take over the functions formerly held by the Secretary of the Continental Congress, some members of Congress urged a fourth executive department, a Home Department headed by a Secretary of the United States for the Home Department. Since many other members considered the proposed office unnecessary and the whole idea thus met with scant favor, a compromise emerged whereby those functions that did not fall easily within the scope of the Treasury and War departments would be assigned to the Department of Foreign Affairs. The result was a law of September 15, 1789, that changed the name of the Department of Foreign Affairs to the Department of State, with its principal officer known as the Secretary of State.

In addition to his responsibilities in the conduct of foreign relations, the Secretary of State now acquired specific domestic duties, such as having custody of the Great Seal and responsibility for publishing the laws enacted by Congress. Thus, what had formerly been the duties of the Secretary for Foreign Affairs under the Confederation government and of the Secretary of the Continental Congress were now combined in those of the Secretary of State.

Since the founding fathers had studied and used the laws establishing the executive offices under the Confederation before creating new ones, it is not surprising that the Secretaryship of State inherited most of the duties and characteristics of its predecessors. There were, however, fundamental differences between the new Secretaryship and the old ones. In the new Federal Government, control over foreign policy was centralized in the President and, under him, in the office of the Secretary of State. The power of final decision in foreign policy, which during the Confederation had belonged to Congress, had now passed to the President.

In theory, the task of the Secretary of State was less difficult than that of the earlier Secretary for Foreign Affairs. The new Secretary, whose main task was to interpret and carry out the foreign policies of the President, was responsible only to one immediate superior, whereas his predecessor had been responsible to many. A strong Secretary of State, as the future would show, might gain such influence with a President that his, in fact, would be the decisive voice in the making of foreign policy, for a Secretary might more easily influence one man than a whole Congress.

Aside from the Secretary of State's complete dependence on the President, a distinctive feature in the founding of his office was that it had not been precisely patterned after models in other governments. Although the Secretaryship of State had European ancestors and a history before it was born, the foreign models that may have influenced its shaping had done their work before 1789. It had grown directly from the experience and precedents of the Confederation era, specifically from the Committee of Secret Correspondence of 1775 and the office of the Secretary of the Continental Congress. No other office in the world was quite comparable to the Secretaryship of State. It came into being as a uniquely American office to meet the specific needs of a new experiment in government.

2

Responsibilities, Powers, Limitations

Although a Secretary of State confers with the President
on important matters of policy and is the President's
agent in the field of foreign relations, in practice he
acts largely on his own initiative and responsibility.
—CORDELL HULL, 1948

FROM the outset, as Congress had intended when it created
his office, the Secretary of State was the nation's highest
appointive executive officer. Thomas Jefferson, the first Secretary
of State, held a vague but nonetheless real priority over the other
department heads in what was to become the Cabinet. Since
Jefferson's time, the Secretary of State has been entitled to take,
and has usually taken, his oath of office before all other members
of the Cabinet.

The Secretary of State's power does not derive, of course, from
protocol. It comes from his influence with the President, from
his ability to persuade the President and guide him properly,
from his role as the President's chief staff adviser, and from his
position as the only Cabinet officer who can devote his full time
to foreign affairs. Next to the President himself, the Secretary
has the heaviest responsibility for defending and promoting the
nation's interests abroad. To do so effectively, he must, besides
carrying out his other responsibilities, keep the American people
aware of the nature of foreign policy and its objectives. He
stands at the center of a web of constitutional, political, and
administrative responsibilities at home that he must fulfill and

defend against encroachment by other executive agencies that also deal with foreign relations. His position of primacy has long roots.

Tradition and the practice of Presidents have strengthened both the Secretary's official precedence and his *de facto* primacy. George Washington told Jefferson that the Secretary of State headed a "higher department" than did the Secretary of the Treasury. At another time, when incensed over certain allegations by Edmund Randolph, the second Secretary of State, whom he had forced to resign, Washington declared that "I made him Secretary of State, placing him at the head of my official council. . . . He occupied the chief seat among the guests at my table."

More than a century and a half later, in 1950, the question of precedence came up under unique circumstances. General George C. Marshall, who had earlier been Secretary of State, returned to Harry S. Truman's Cabinet as Secretary of Defense. Dean G. Acheson, who had been Under Secretary of State during Marshall's tenure, was now Secretary of State. "To all of us it was natural and proper," Acheson wrote, "that next to the President deference was due to General Marshall. But he [Marshall] would have none of it. The Secretary of State was the senior officer to whom he punctiliously deferred, not only in matters of protocol but in council as well." This practice was also in keeping with the view of President Truman himself, who believed that "the most important Cabinet officer is the Secretary of State."

Most Secretaries of State have been sensitive about the preeminence of their office. Edward Livingston, Andrew Jackson's second Secretary of State, was delighted with the prestige of his post. "Here I am," he wrote a month after becoming Secretary, "in the second place in the United States—some say the first. . . ."

Other Secretaries have gained satisfaction from the fact that on social and ceremonial occasions they took precedence over their Cabinet colleagues and others. Mrs. James G. Blaine, particularly, was pleased that her husband's position placed him socially above all but the President. Shortly after her husband had accepted the offer to serve at the head of James A. Garfield's Cabinet, Mrs. Blaine wrote to one of her sons that "all the world is paying court to the coming or expected Secretary of State. Socially you know it is about the best position."

The traditional pre-eminence of the Secretary of State was enhanced by a law of January 19, 1886, that made him second, after the Vice-President, in line in the Presidential succession, followed according to rank by other members of the Cabinet. Even though a new law of July 18, 1947, has placed the Speaker of the House and the President Pro Tempore of the Senate ahead of the Secretary of State, he still outranks the other department heads in the line of succession.

John Hay was twice the direct heir to the Presidency—after the death of Vice-President Garret A. Hobart, in November, 1899, and again after the assassination of William McKinley, in September, 1901. Stressing the Secretary of State's Cabinet rank, the newspapers referred to him as "the senior member" and the "ranking member" of the Cabinet. Theodore Roosevelt, the new President, made a special point of Hay's place in the Presidential succession by leaving him at the seat of the government while he himself accompanied McKinley's funeral party to Canton, Ohio. Since "I am the next heir to the Presidency," Hay explained, "he did not want too many eggs in the same Pullman car."

It is evident that in prestige, influence, and often even in power, the Secretary of State has long ranked second only to the President. Even so prominent and active a Vice-President as Richard M. Nixon had less stature than Secretary of State John Foster Dulles. Yet in the pay he receives and the legal authority that is his, the Secretary of State is not superior to the other members of the Cabinet. He is only the first among equals. Even in his own domain of foreign affairs, his voice has no greater authority than that of his Cabinet colleagues, unless the President decides that it should. Under Washington, for example, Alexander Hamilton, the Secretary of the Treasury, was the most influential member of the Cabinet, even in matters of foreign policy. His views usually carried more weight than did those of the Secretary of State.

One hundred fifty years later, in the relationship between Franklin D. Roosevelt and Cordell Hull, the same principle held. Roosevelt distrusted the Department of State, believing it incapable of conducting the nation's foreign relations during a time of crisis in the manner he desired. Secretary of State Hull, hence, attained less influence in the government, even in the conduct of foreign relations, than did some of Roosevelt's other advisers. Clearly, in the influence the Secretary of State wields in practice, he is not always the foremost Cabinet officer. His precedence may at times be little more than an expression of protocol.

Nonetheless, over the years the Secretaryship of State has grown steadily in importance, in part because the foreign relations of the United States have vastly increased, and in part because the power and influence of the Presidency itself have expanded. The Secretary of State is so close to the President that virtually any important development that affects the powers of the Presidency affects his powers too. By law, practice, and tradition, the Secretaryship of State is the office controlled most closely and directly by the President. It is, therefore, more an extension of the Presidency itself than are the other executive departments.

Explicitly, two of the basic functions of the Secretary of State are to assist the President in formulating foreign policy and to carry it out through the channels of the Department of State. Harry Truman, more than most Presidents, emphasized this role of the Secretary. In his view:

> The function of the Secretary of State is to be the President's personal adviser on foreign affairs. He has to run a department which should have skilled and experienced men to get the best information possible on any subject or problem that affects the relations with other governments. The Secretary of State obtains, if he can, the very best advice from the people who live with the problems of foreign affairs so that he may present it to the President.

Others who have worked closely with the Secretary have stressed the same responsibilities. "Ideally," a Chairman of the Senate Committee on Foreign Relations said, "the secretary of state should be the best-posted man in the country on foreign relations; he should keep the President apprised of what is going on abroad and he should advise him on formulating policies." In accord with the President's views, the Secretary should usually carry, in addition, the burden of high-level negotiations with other governments.

Technically, then, the Secretary of State is the President's chief adviser in foreign affairs and the department head responsible for matters related to them. Under certain conditions, he can be, as Truman implied, virtually the President's personal secretary in charge of foreign affairs. That, in effect, was Bainbridge Colby's status as Woodrow Wilson's Secretary of State.

Some Secretaries, however, have looked upon their relationship to the President as being a more impersonal connection. Henry L. Stimson, a Secretary of State with a flair for things military, and George C. Marshall, a soldier, viewed their relationship to the President as that of a soldier to a commanding officer. Even though they might disagree with their chief and might not like his orders, they would, like good soldiers, carry out his wishes.

Probably no Secretary of State has analyzed his relationship to the President, his own status, and the responsibilities of his office as thoroughly as did John Foster Dulles. He left a record of his analysis in a memorandum headed "More Important Duties of Secretary of State." Although the memorandum's sixteen points do not cover all the responsibilities of the modern Secretary, they do offer a useful and representative summary of what his job encompasses.

Dulles listed protocol first, pointing out that the Secretary of State has to meet foreign chiefs of state and foreign ministers when they come to Washington. Second, he must receive foreign ambassadors and accept their statements on matters pertaining to relations between their countries and the United States. Third, the Secretary has to visit foreign countries and attend international conferences connected with the United Nations, the North Atlantic Treaty Organization, security in the Pacific, and other matters. Fourth, he selects personnel for the highest posts in the State Department and the foreign missions.

In the fifth point, Dulles considered relations with Congress, receiving its members and testifying before its committees. Sixth, the Secretary has to prepare speeches for himself—and for the President, when they deal with foreign affairs. Dulles' seventh point concerned public relations, that is, the Secretary's press conferences and private meetings with newspapermen and radio commentators. Eighth, to maintain morale within the State Department, he said, the Secretary has to consult with his top-level associates and diplomats who have returned to the United States on leave. He listed social functions as the ninth item, pointing out that the Secretary has to attend dinners and receptions given by the diplomatic corps and American officials.

According to Dulles' tenth point, the Secretary of State has to establish policies for dealing and settling controversies with independent coordinate agencies, such as the departments of Defense, Treasury, and Commerce, and the Central Intelligence Agency, all of which are also concerned with foreign relations. The Secretary has to approve important outgoing cables and read important incoming ones as well as the memoranda of significant departmental conversations. In addition, he has to give personal attention to a portion of the department's correspondence and see at least some of the people who demand to speak to a top official.

Dulles' final three points touch on duties he considered most significant, those that involve the making of policy. The Secretary has to attend Cabinet meetings and general talks at the White House, consult with the President, and keep him informed of developments in foreign affairs. He also has to deal with crises that may arise suddenly anywhere on the globe and call for immediate reactions by the government, and lastly, he has to formulate long-range policies.

All Dulles' points relate to what he called "the Secretary's foreign policy functions," for only that, the most important feature of the Secretaryship, interested him. He wished to concentrate on the making of policy and had no interest in the Secretary's domestic responsibilities. These duties may often be delegated, but the foreign-policy function usually cannot. There is no substitute for the influence and authority of the Secretary of State in the meetings of the Cabinet. This is also true of the National Security Council, a special advisory body which is used by the President to coordinate foreign and defense policies and which often formulates basic decisions in foreign policy. No one else, moreover, can explain the Secretary's views to the President as well as he can himself or replace him in his relations with the President.

Another factor in the Secretary's job that Dulles did not emphasize, but of which he was acutely aware, is the obligation to reconcile the demands of foreign policy with those of domestic politics when the two seem to be, or are, in conflict. This calls for considerable finesse, a quality that few Secretaries of recent years have had in great measure. Without meeting this obligation, the Secretary may not be able to do full justice to all the responsibilities of his office.

The President needs a strong Secretary of State, one who is familiar with domestic as well as international politics, one who can carry his share of responsibility in dealing with Congress. John F. Kennedy, a President who has had long experience in Congress, has stated that he considers it imperative for a Secretary of State to be able to get along well with Congress. The relations of any Secretary with Congress so condition the degree to which he can execute his foreign policy that he has an obligation to gain the confidence of Congress. His effectiveness in dealing with Congress, of course, can be no greater than the strength of the support he inspires in the nation, which, in turn, depends largely on the President's own strength politically.

This does not, however, relieve the Secretary of the responsibility of marshaling public opinion in support of himself and his policies. He must, in fact, become master of these domestic political responsibilities before he can become truly successful in the management of foreign policy.

I.

The chief limitation on the Secretary of State is that he, like other Cabinet officers, has no special claim to consultation with the President, even in matters relating solely to foreign affairs. The President is under no obligation, legal or moral, to consult with him on issues of foreign policy, and the Secretary can claim no right to participate in the decisions affecting those issues. Yet, according to Dean Acheson, if the President "is to perform his duties in the wisest and most effective way, his Secretary of State must be his principal adviser in this field. The President will, and should, seek advice from whatever quarters he wishes. He will consult with and listen to many persons. But the Secretary of State should be privy to all his thoughts and to him should be given the last clear chance for advice before action."

At times, however, the President has not given the Secretary of State even the chance to offer information on foreign policy, let alone advice. If another member of the Cabinet interferes with foreign policy and the President supports him, the Secretary is almost helpless to prevent the invasion of his area of responsibility. This occurred in the original Cabinet, when Hamilton's meddling with foreign affairs infuriated Jefferson, and again a century later, when Benjamin Harrison's Secretary of the Navy, in a dispute with Chile, dictated a policy virtually the opposite of that advised by the then Secretary of State, James G. Blaine.

No President, however, so frequently undercut the authority of his Secretary of State as did Franklin D. Roosevelt. Assistant Secretary of State Raymond Moley was the first confidential adviser who had a weightier role in formulating a specific foreign policy than did Cordell Hull. Moley reported directly to Roosevelt, often without Hull's knowledge. At the World Economic Conference, held in London in 1933, Moley, acting as the President's personal agent, overshadowed and humiliated Hull.

None of the President's advisers, however, angered Hull quite as much as did Sumner Welles, the Assistant Secretary of State in charge of Latin American affairs. Roosevelt had brought Welles, an old friend, into the White House inner circle while at the same time excluding Hull. Once Hull told a Cabinet colleague that although he regularly spoke to the President by telephone, he seldom saw him. Welles, he pointed out, saw Roosevelt daily.

Hull later charged that Welles "abused his trust by going over my head to see the President without instructions from me and undertaking in one way or another virtually to act as Secretary of State." For instance, in the preparations for the Atlantic Conference, held in August, 1941, off the coast of Newfoundland, between Prime Minister Winston Churchill and Roosevelt, Hull had no part, but Welles did. Hull, in fact, did not learn of the conference until Welles told him.

Welles continually slighted Hull and acted as if he were the President's personal assistant, not amenable to the authority of the Secretary of State. In his memoirs, Hull explained with understandable bitterness:

Welles was carrying on personal correspondence with our diplomats and with officials of other Governments which should have been carried on through the official channels of the State Department. He was sending personal notes to them and inviting personal responses from them on matters calling for Department notes handled in the regular way. The adverse effect of this was that he was gathering into his own hands items of negotiation or discussion that should have been of more general knowledge to me and to the Department officers directly concerned.

Hull also clashed with other department heads when they encroached on what he considered his exclusive domain. Several of them took a hand in foreign affairs because they knew that the President sometimes refused to accept Hull's ideas and would listen to and perhaps even act upon their own suggestions. Henry

A. Wallace, at one time Secretary of Agriculture and then Vice-President; Harold L. Ickes, Secretary of the Interior; and Henry Morgenthau, Jr., Secretary of the Treasury, were, Hull asserted, the most frequent trespassers on his field of responsibility.

Acting as the President's own representative, Vice-President Wallace took several special trips abroad, going to Latin America in 1943 and China in 1944. Those missions irked the Secretary of State. "I never at any time favored excursions into foreign affairs by Wallace," Hull wrote. "I was convinced that no person outside the State Department and the White House could break into these affairs without serious risk of running amuck, so to speak, and causing hurtful complications."

In trying to defend his jurisdiction, the Secretary of State clashed more often with Morgenthau than with any other Cabinet colleague. According to Hull, Morgenthau "often acted as if he were clothed with authority to project himself into the field of foreign affairs and inaugurate efforts to shape the course of foreign policy in given instances." Hull believed that the Secretary of the Treasury seldom lost an opportunity to meddle in foreign relations. He even conducted negotiations with foreign governments, Hull charged, "which were the function of the State Department." Morgenthau's plan for reducing postwar Germany to an agricultural state, which Hull opposed, and his work in "inducing the President to accept it without consultation with the State Department was," the Secretary of State said, "an outstanding instance of this interference."

Another limitation of the Secretaryship, one that has made a marked impression on foreigners, is the influence frequently exercised upon foreign affairs by unofficial Presidential advisers. Those advisers, in effect, displace the Secretary of State as the President's foremost consultant in the making of foreign policy. Secretaries who have been confronted with the problem of the unofficial adviser have seldom been happy about it. Regardless of how a President or anyone else may gloss over the status of the personal adviser, his mere existence reflects a lack of confidence in the Secretary of State.

Ulysses S. Grant, for example, had a penchant for old military cronies and kept some of them around the White House. Having direct access to the President, they would at times persuade him to embark on dubious ventures in foreign affairs, sometimes without consulting his Secretary of State, Hamilton Fish. Outraged, particularly by the influence of General Orville Babcock, Grant's private secretary, Fish protested the continual interference of the unofficial Grant family in his department and threatened to resign. He told the President:

> The State Department, above all others, cannot be administered except with the most unreserved confidence given to its head by the Executive. When that confidence is shaken, or when the influence of the head of the Department in the administration of its affairs, or the formation of its policy, is overshadowed by others, a sensible or a sensitive man will appreciate that the time for his retirement has arrived.

Fish thus made clear a basic principle governing the power of the Secretary of State. The Secretary can function best as a high government official only when he has behind him the President's confidence, personal influence, and prestige, when there is no man or other influence between the President and himself.

Fish demanded control over matters pertaining to his department, which, he said, is "necessary not only to a confident and satisfactory discharge of the delicate and complicated duties of the office, but also to the independence of feeling without which the high position which I have held in your Administration cannot be worthily occupied." There must be, he added, assurance "of the withdrawal of this Army influence—this back-stairs, Kitchen-Cabinet control over the affairs of my Department."

Grant gave the required assurance, saying there would be no more interference in Fish's domain, because he admired and needed Fish. The Secretary of State, therefore, by threatening to resign, was able to maintain control over the conduct of foreign policy. This is unusual; as a rule, Presidents who have resorted to unofficial advisers in foreign policy have been those who distrusted or had little confidence in their Secretaries of State. This principle can be seen in the cases of Secretaries who had to deal with two of the most noted of the unofficial advisers, Colonel Edward M. House and Harry Hopkins.

II.

Colonel House, a close friend of Woodrow Wilson, had direct access to him, enjoyed his confidence, acted as an executive agent, and exerted a greater influence over the formulation of foreign policy than did Secretaries of State William Jennings Bryan or Robert Lansing. House, not the Secretaries, usually acted as the President's most effective counselor and also as an unofficial spokesman in matters of foreign policy. So close was House to the President that at times it was difficult to distinguish House's ideas from those of Wilson.

House's unique power had grown in part out of Wilson's lack of confidence in his Secretaries of State. Apparently, the President could never fully overcome his feelings that Bryan was not competent to deal with great matters of state. At one time after World War I had begun, the President refused to trust Bryan even to act as the ordinary channel of communication between himself and the European belligerents. Without consulting his Secretary of State, Wilson sent House as his personal emissary on a peace mission to the belligerent capitals. When Bryan finally learned of the mission from House, he was keenly disappointed and probably deeply hurt.

Since Wilson and House shut out Bryan from important areas of foreign affairs, sometimes leaving him only with routine administrative duties within the State Department, it was natural that the Secretary resented House and his own humiliating status. Bryan accepted his subordination to House because, other than to resign, he could do little about it.

When Lansing succeeded Bryan in the Secretaryship, House continued as the President's intimate adviser. House, in fact, had urged Lansing's appointment partly because Lansing knew of his own relationship to the President and "tacitly accepted existing conditions."

Even though House continued to handle critical diplomatic negotiations for the President, the new Secretary of State gave no outward sign of resenting House's privileged position. "I bow to the political astuteness of Colonel House in most things," Lansing recorded in his diary. House himself apparently never detected resentment and usually found Lansing willing to co-operate with him. "I shall always remember with gratitude his attitude toward me," House wrote in later years, "for my position was unusual and without precedent, and it would have been natural for him to object to my ventures in his sphere of activities. He never did. He was willing for me to help in any way the President thought best."

Perhaps more powerful than House in matters of foreign policy was Harry Hopkins, Franklin D. Roosevelt's intimate adviser. Hopkins, a former social worker, was one of those "radical" New Dealers whom Secretary of State Hull disliked. While working for the New Deal, Hopkins had won Roosevelt's friendship and confidence in a way no one else had succeeded in doing since the death of Louis M. Howe, an earlier political adviser, in 1936.

In 1940, Hopkins moved into the White House, where he had well-nigh instant access to the President. "That kind of propinquity," another Roosevelt adviser wrote, "which enabled [him] to see the President at almost any time, was the greatest possible assurance of influence and power." Hull, in contrast, sometimes went weeks without a glimpse of the President.

During the last five years of Roosevelt's life, Hopkins was usually his most influential adviser in foreign affairs; he was called "Roosevelt's own personal Foreign Office." Hopkins even attended Cabinet meetings. He, not the Secretary of State, seemed to provide the readiest means of informal contact with foreign dignitaries and with the President himself in questions of foreign policy. Yet he had no legal status. He was only a private citizen without office, rank, or pay.

More than had Colonel House, Hopkins came to symbolize

the great personal power of the President in foreign relations and the insignificant role of the Secretary of State under certain conditions. Roosevelt gave Hopkins broad powers of decision in foreign policy, powers he denied his Secretary of State, because he liked and trusted Hopkins. While Hull bored the President with his solemn cautiousness, Hopkins, even more than Welles, was quick, direct, and bold in attacking a problem. That approach suited Roosevelt, who, in his lofty and lonely responsibility, felt the need of advice from someone whose judgment he trusted. Never being close to the President, Hull could not fill that need for informal personal advice suited to Roosevelt's patterns of thought. More than any of Roosevelt's other advisers in foreign affairs, Harry Hopkins was able to do so.

Unofficial advisers and official subordinates, such as Hopkins and Welles, are able at times to overshadow the Secretary of State in the shaping of foreign policy, not because of any inherent or technical flaw in the Secretaryship but because of the tremendous flexibility in the powers of the office, and, of course, in the Presidency itself. This flexibility, in fact, is a distinctive feature of the Secretaryship, one that we shall refer to again.

Roosevelt's informal advisers in foreign policy did not necessarily usurp the Secretary's jurisdiction; at times, they merely filled a vacuum. Since the President often did not use his Secretary in formulating important policies, Hopkins, Welles, Morgenthau, and others stepped in and supplied the counsel that might under other circumstances have come from the Secretary of State. This illustrates what is almost a truism—that a Secretary can make his greatest contribution to important decisions only if the President accepts and uses him as his chief agent in foreign affairs.

Hull himself attributed his awkward status to the fact that he was never a member of Roosevelt's inner circle and, hence, was at a disadvantage in defending his domain from assaults within the Administration. He believed also that the President did not consult him enough and allowed other officials to attack State Department policies, and that he himself had to fight for his department's policies without the President's backing. There is considerable truth in Hull's observation, for if the President makes it an obvious practice to consult the Secretary of State and uphold him in conflicts over policy, the other Cabinet officers are likely to accept the Secretary's *de facto* primacy.

Hull's, and hence the Secretary of State's, subordination during World War II is remarkable only because of the extremes to which Roosevelt went to keep important matters of foreign policy out of his hands. During wars, Secretaries of State have at times lost importance relative to the warmaking departments and have had few opportunities to bask in the limelight. The Presidents have retained a close control over foreign policy and the military men have won the glory and the public esteem. During the War of 1812, James Monroe, for instance, believed that he had little more to do than to write instructions to representatives abroad and care for routine administrative matters, and hence he became dissatisfied with the Secretaryship.

William H. Seward is an exception to the pattern of wartime impotence, but he was Secretary of State during a civil war, when the President's main energies were devoted to the domestic battles. Seward's power and influence, moreover, derived not solely from the fact that Abraham Lincoln had delegated broad powers to him in the area of foreign relations but also from his own status as the dominant personality in the Cabinet.

At times, the Secretary of State's power may be limited by the nature of the Cabinet. Unlike cabinets in parliamentary governments, the President's Cabinet does not have collective responsibility and is not a council of political colleagues. It is, instead, essentially a council of advisers, whose existence and influence depend on the will of the President. The foreign policies emanating from this purely Presidential institution become significant in terms of national policy only because the President chooses to adopt them. Since neither the Constitution nor Congress created the Cabinet, it has no legal status. It came into existence under President Washington as an experiment within the scope of his broad constitutional powers over his department heads. Its status, therefore, is anchored in tradition.

Some Presidents, such as Washington and Truman, discussed important issues of foreign policy in Cabinet meetings, often asked the department heads to vote on decisions affecting those issues, and acted upon the majority's wishes. Washington gave the Secretary of State's vote the same weight as that of the other department heads even in matters pertaining to foreign affairs. That procedure explains in part why Hamilton, who dominated the Cabinet, was able to direct foreign policy.

Under such conditions, the Secretary of State has no way of controlling foreign policy. Unlike a foreign minister in a parliamentary government, or even his predecessor in the Confederation Government, he cannot take his case to the national legislature and there explain or defend his policies. If the President uses the Cabinet to shape decisions in foreign policy, the Secretary, as a department head, has to make his case in the Cabinet. Otherwise, as is usually the procedure, he has to make it directly with the President.

Since the Secretary of State is not a responsible minister heading a foreign office, his actions and decisions must reflect the President's views, or if policy originates with the Secretary, his views must be accepted by the President as his own. In September, 1946, when Secretary of Commerce Henry A. Wallace publicly attacked the foreign policy that Secretary of State James F. Byrnes was carrying out, Byrnes protested in the name of the above principle. He asked President Truman to restrain Wallace, as a member of the Cabinet, from openly criticizing his policy, saying that "whoever is Secretary of State must be known to have the undivided support of your administration." Later, in the case of Dean Acheson, there was never any doubt that the Secretary of State was the President's spokesman in foreign affairs, for Truman went out of his way to support Acheson despite bitter attacks against him.

Truman had to defend his Secretary of State, for any foreign policy, whether it originates with the Secretary or whether he acts merely as an agent in carrying it out, becomes the President's policy. Technically, the Secretary of State has no policies of his own. All policies must be presented as coming from the President. When a Secretary does formulate a policy, it is assumed to have the President's support, for the President, as the founding fathers had intended, is officially responsible for the acts of his department head.

The Secretary of State, it must be emphasized, is the representative of the President—and not of the people directly—when carrying out foreign policy; the President—not the Secretary—is responsible to the people. No Secretary of State, as a result, can match the role of the President in the conduct of foreign relations, for no Secretary, regardless of how capable, can assume the authority of the President in representing the people and the nation.

III.

Since the Secretary of State acts in the President's name, it is virtually an unwritten rule that Secretaries who do not agree with the President must nevertheless carry out his policies faithfully or resign. In fact, mere want of mutual confidence can offer sufficient cause for a Secretary's dismissal.

Secretary of State Timothy Pickering, for instance, had no respect for John Adams. When Adams' foreign policy did not agree with Pickering's own ideas, he attempted to thwart it. Adams tried to force him to resign, but Pickering refused. The President then dismissed him. After that, the unwritten principle became so firmly established that although subsequent Secretaries of State have been forced from office because of disagreements with the President, none since Pickering has been fired outright. In no case since Pickering's, moreover, has a Secretary of State set out openly and deliberately to sabotage the foreign policy of his chief.

Although President Wilson accused Robert Lansing of disloyalty and forced him to resign, Lansing had not attempted to wreck the President's policies. Wilson demanded his Secretary's resignation because he realized that Lansing carried out his policies reluctantly, because his judgment differed from Wilson's, and Wilson preferred a Secretary of State whose mind would willingly go along with his own.

Lansing had subordinated his own judgments because Wilson cast aside or seldom solicited his opinions, even on issues of foreign policy. He had not attempted to resign earlier because he did not wish to give the impression of deserting the President in a time of crisis, but when Wilson demanded his resignation, he grasped the opportunity with a sense of relief because it finally freed him from the responsibility of having to carry out policies he disliked. "In hiding my feelings and subordinating my judgment I have felt a hypocrite," he confessed to his diary, "possibly I have been one, but what else could I do in these extraordinary conditions?"

Like Hull's, Lansing's ineffectiveness was unusual, for Secretaries of State more often have had broad responsibilities and have not been expected to confine their advice to foreign affairs. Most Presidents have invited their views on domestic matters as well. Such Secretaries as Martin Van Buren, William M. Evarts, and Jeremiah S. Black, in fact, were more valuable to Presidents Andrew Jackson, Rutherford B. Hayes, and James Buchanan, respectively, as political advisers than as managers of foreign relations.

Secretary of State Seward, too, under both Lincoln and Andrew Johnson, was more than a manager of foreign affairs. He helped write Lincoln's inaugural address, took a hand in military matters, worked on problems of internal security, and offered counsel on all kinds of domestic issues. He advised President Johnson on domestic politics and problems of Reconstruction and wrote some of his veto messages. And in the twentieth century, William H. Taft also relied on his Secretary of State, Philander C. Knox, for advice on internal as well as foreign affairs.

Some Presidents have relied so heavily on their Secretaries of State that instead of giving their own direction to foreign policy, they have accepted direction from their Secretaries. Such Secretarial dominance has usually come when a President has not been interested in diplomatic negotiations and the shaping of foreign policies, or when he has been beset by so many other problems that he has not been able to devote needed time to foreign affairs. Under these and similar conditions, if left to his own devices and if able, the Secretary of State has decided what matters shall be presented to the President for consideration, decision, or acquiescence. Such conditions prevailed during the Secretaryships of Daniel Webster under Tyler, Hamilton Fish under Grant, Charles E. Hughes under Harding, and John Foster Dulles under Eisenhower.

Fish's dominance, in view of his difficulty with back-stairs advisers, is particularly noteworthy. At the end of eight years, when he finally gave up his Secretaryship, he was recognized by contemporaries as the man who had virtually run the government and as the ablest of the twenty-five men who had held Cabinet posts under Grant. Far more than most Secretaries, he had won the President's confidence, the essential factor in the power of a strong Secretary of State. So highly did Grant come to esteem his Secretary of State that before he left the White House, he wrote a letter advising the nomination of Fish for President in case of a deadlock at the Republican convention. On a later occasion, when a friend listed those whom he considered the three greatest statesmen of the age, Grant insisted on adding a fourth—Hamilton Fish.

Dulles' dominance came during the tense years of the Cold War, years of seemingly perpetual crisis in foreign policy, years when the power of the Secretary of State seemed magnified beyond what it had been in the past, years when the President leaned heavily on him for guidance. Harry Truman gave his Secretaries of State considerable freedom, but President Eisenhower went beyond him. Although he never abdicated his power of final decision, he usually followed the practice of "leaving it to Foster," meaning that, in most instances, Dulles had practically a free hand in the conduct of foreign relations.

Eisenhower was convinced that Dulles had the ability and

experience to handle foreign policy as he, the President, wished it. He believed that since he had given his trust to Dulles in the first place, he should look to his Secretary for ideas and outlines of policy. Like Grant, Eisenhower had an almost boundless admiration for his Secretary, saying that Dulles had his unqualified support, behaved himself "like a master," supplied the heart and brains in the formulation of foreign policy, and was the greatest Secretary of State in the history of the nation. Few Presidents have relied as heavily on their Secretaries of State as did Eisenhower on Dulles. In effect, Dulles formulated foreign policy and Eisenhower made it his own.

Like John Quincy Adams and Seward, Dulles was a strong Secretary of State who dramatized his own status and hence the Secretaryship. A few days after taking over the State Department, Dulles spoke to the nation by radio and television, attempting to add stature to the Secretaryship and to gain public confidence by assuring the people that he would be devoted to their welfare. "You needn't be afraid," he said, "that we're working against you and for others." That broadcast, Dulles believed, was necessary, because the Secretary's prestige, owing to a situation he had inherited from Acheson, was at a low ebb and needed bolstering.

Unlike Truman, who had resented Byrnes's efforts to capture public attention, Eisenhower did not mind Dulles' frequent attempts to gain publicity and even seemed to encourage them. One of the distinctive features of Dulles' Secretaryship, in fact, was his frequent use of radio and television to talk directly to the American people. He was the most widely advertised Secretary of State in the nation's history. One friendly critic quipped that he used an Assistant Secretary of State as his personal press agent.

Again like John Quincy Adams and Seward, Dulles seems to have craved public approval, to have been keenly conscious of his place in history, and to have striven consciously to make a record. This can be seen in a special interview he granted to a reporter for *Life* magazine in January, 1956. The article, based on recorded conversations, portrayed Dulles as the Administration's genius, who valiantly preserved the peace after bringing the nation to the brink of war. The Secretary of State, it said, had given the nation "the greatest display of personal diplomacy since the great days of the Franklin-Adams-Jefferson triumvirate in the Europe of the 1790's"—a claim that Dulles did not deny.

Critics have pointed out that Dulles claimed too much and hence, in effect, revived an old argument running as follows: Since the Secretary of State is the President's instrument, all credit for achievement in foreign policy belongs to the President. Among those who have refused to accept such an assumption was Theodore Roosevelt, a vigorous Chief Executive who himself dominated the conduct of foreign relations. He wrote:

> To deny [Secretary of State Elihu] Root credit for what the Department of State has done because it has been done under me as President is a good deal like denying credit to Sherman and Sheridan because they were under Grant. The President is of course responsible for the general policy of the administration in foreign affairs, and here and there or now and then he must himself work out some given problem. . . . But in most things done by the State Department it is the Secretary of State, if he is a man like Root, who does practically all the work.

Some Secretaries, particularly the brilliant John Quincy Adams, have chafed under the knowledge that most of the credit for accomplishment in foreign affairs goes to the President. Adams feared that even though he had conceived the idea of extending the nation's boundary to the Pacific and had persuaded President James Monroe to act upon that idea, he would not get credit for it. "I record the first assertion of this claim for the United States as my own," he wrote in his diary, "because it is known to be mine perhaps only to members of the present Administration, and may perhaps never be known to the public."

From Adams' brain came most of the basic ideas in the foreign policy of the Monroe Administrations, and he executed the diplomacy that carried them out. He helped shape the Monroe

Doctrine, negotiated with Spain's Don Luis de Onís the treaty of 1819 that transferred to the United States both Florida and Spain's claim to a domain on the Pacific, and, in 1824, completed a treaty with Russia that recognized the American claim to the Oregon country. He could boast with considerable justification that "of the public history of Mr. Monroe's administration, all that will be worth telling to posterity hitherto has been transacted through the Department of State."

Strong Secretaries like Adams, Fish, and Dulles were in command of foreign policy, initiated it, built it up, and carried it out. Dulles, despite the controversy that swirled about him, was identified the world over as the master of American foreign policy more often than any other Secretary of State. Even Adams did not possess his far-flung influence.

The reasons for this are simple enough. Monroe did not surrender to Adams the extensive powers that Eisenhower ceded to Dulles, and the United States of Adams' day cannot be compared to the powerful nation of the 1950's committed to a world-wide network of alliances.

Nonetheless, whether it be Adams in the "era of good feelings" or Dulles in the era of hurtling missiles, the tenure of the strong Secretaries shows that the Secretaryship of State has been and can be an office of impressive power. Some Secretaries have even been surprised by the extent of their power. "I was not aware," John C. Calhoun told his daughter shortly after becoming Secretary of State, "until I took charge of the State Dept. of the immense influence, which may be exerted through it on foreign and domestic relations." The responsibilities, powers, and limitations of the Secretaryship, in other words, are so flexible that the office can sometimes bring frustration, but more often an eminence second only to that of the President.

3

Qualifications and Selection

> . . . a Secretary of State ought to have pierced into the
> remotest Periods of ancient Times and into the most
> Distant Regions of the Earth: He should have studied
> the Map of Man, in his savage as well as civilized State.
> It is more necessary that a Secretary of State should be
> omniscient, than a President, provided the President
> be honest and judicious. Where can we find such Men?
> either for Presidents or Secretaries?
>
> —JOHN ADAMS, 1811

IN practice, there are no formal qualifications for the Secretaryship, no technique or special training that would prepare one, and no standard of selection. Presidents and Presidents-elect have followed no rules and have selected their Secretaries of State for many varying reasons. Some have appointed personal friends, a few have sought good administrators, but most have chosen their Cabinet heads to hold or gain political support for their Administrations. Seldom has a President appointed a Secretary solely because he sought an adviser trained and experienced in diplomacy and the handling of foreign affairs.

As a result, when a man gains the Secretaryship it usually comes to him as an interlude in a career that has had little to do with foreign affairs, and not as the culmination or even an integral part of a professional career—a pattern different from that in the parliamentary system. In Great Britain, for instance, where the Foreign Secretary comes from Parliament and remains a part of it, the portfolio for foreign affairs can be the goal toward which a member of Parliament constantly moves. If and when he reaches that objective, it usually crowns a lifelong political career devoted to foreign affairs.

Disturbed by this lack of professional requirements, some men who have studied the Secretaryship have suggested qualifications. It should be kept in mind, however, that the selection of a Secretary in each instance involves a specific man, not an abstract principle.

John Adams, in the years of his retirement, wrote that the Secretary of State "ought to be a Man of universal Reading in Laws, Governments, History. Our whole terrestrial Universe ought to be summarily comprehended in his Mind." Adams even suggested that the Secretary should be more knowledgeable than the President.

Others have suggested qualifications less lofty but more obtainable. A Secretary of State, some have said, should be versed in international law, in the practice and procedure of diplomacy, should have a firm grasp of American foreign policy, and should know other peoples, especially from travel in foreign lands.

Some have argued that such professional qualifications are unimportant. Within proper limits, they insist, experience in domestic politics is more important, even essential. Since most problems a Secretary of State has to face are inherently political, he needs political perspective, insight, and wisdom more than technical training. In his relations with the President, Congress, and other members of the Administration, it has been pointed out, the Secretary has to deal with politicians. In selecting a Secretary of State, therefore, a President could rightly give more weight to political than to diplomatic experience, to ability and sound judgment than to specialized knowledge. The lawyer with political training who has risen to party chieftain and has been a candidate for high office, one student of the Secretaryship wrote, is well qualified for the post. Dean Acheson said that in selecting a Secretary, a President should simply be guided by his belief that the man he wants is the one who can help him more than any other in dealing with the problems he foresees.

Those who stress law and politics are moving with the tide of history, for most Secretaries of State have been lawyers or men who have had some legal training. This fact reveals something of the true nature of the office. From the beginning of the national government, the legal profession has offered the likeliest path to political preferment, and from the beginning, the alliance of law and politics has dominated the Secretaryship.

Most Secretaries have come from the higher ranks of political life, having been selected primarily for their status in the party controlling the executive branch of the government. More often than not they have come to the office possessing little experience in, or even knowledge of, world affairs. Although the main concern of the Secretaryship of State is foreign relations, the office is essentially political.

No one—not even men with considerable diplomatic experience, such as James Monroe, John Quincy Adams, or John Hay —has risen to the Secretaryship by virtue of having selected diplomacy as a career. No professional diplomat, in other words, has ever been Secretary of State, though John W. Foster, who served less than seven months, was an expert in international law and diplomatic practice. John Foster Dulles, too, had steeped himself in diplomatic experience but was not a career diplomat. Christian A. Herter had been a Foreign Service Officer, but with him, as with most of the others, political connections, not his training in and knowledge of diplomacy, had been decisive in his selection.

Most Secretaries have had political experience, generally in national affairs, before taking office. George Marshall, the only professional soldier to hold the Secretaryship, is the most familiar exception to this rule. He considered himself a nonpartisan Secretary of State, though he served a Democratic Administration, and even urged the appointment of a Republican as his successor so as to perpetuate the bipartisan foreign policy he had administered. Although President Truman deeply admired

Marshall and often followed his suggestions virtually without question, he did not do so in this instance and thus kept inviolate one of the most enduring traditions of the Secretaryship—that the Secretary of State must not come from the opposition party.

While it is true that Washington and Jefferson belonged to opposing parties, it should be remembered that when Washington appointed Jefferson to the Secretaryship, national political parties had not yet formed. Since he had been elected unanimously, moreover, Washington did not have to weigh political considerations in selecting his Secretary of State. Believing himself above political strife, the head of a nonpartisan government, he had no intention of selecting a Cabinet on the basis of political harmony.

Before the end of Washington's first term, all this had changed. National political coalitions, the Federalist and Republican parties, were forming under the leadership of his two major department heads, Hamilton and Jefferson. Those two also differed over foreign policy. Hamilton evolved a policy favorable to England, whereas Jefferson desired one friendly to France. Washington's Cabinet, in other words, was seriously split.

As Washington himself became more and more of a Federalist, the split grew deeper, for as Hamilton's ideas were transformed into policy, the Secretary of State found himself administering the foreign policy of a political enemy under the cover of an allegedly nonpartisan Administration. For a while, nonetheless, Jefferson stayed on, the only Secretary of State to carry out faithfully the foreign policy of an Administration to which he was philosophically opposed. He could maintain this unique status because at this early stage of Cabinet growth, there had not yet developed a precedent or clear obligation for a Secretary of State to be politically loyal to the President. As long as he performed his duties with due diligence and carried out policy as the President desired, he was technically free to follow his own political sentiments.

Later, as the Cabinet became an institution, political conformity became a requirement for anyone who would become

Secretary of State. Jefferson's successor, Edmund Randolph, learned this at great cost.

Considering himself a neutral in politics, Randolph told the President when he took over the Secretaryship that "let the consequence be what it may in this perilous office, no consideration of party shall ever influence me. . . ." Despised by both political factions, Randolph soon found neutrality untenable, and like Jefferson, he came to resent and oppose Hamilton's dominance in foreign relations. To Hamiltonians, therefore, he appeared disloyal to the Administration, and since he was the only non-Federalist who still held a high post in the government, they became eager to get rid of him.

In the summer of 1795, on the basis of inconclusive evidence supplied by the British, Randolph's Federalist Cabinet colleagues accused him of disloyalty to his country and the Administration through collusion with Republicans and the French Minister in the United States. Believing the accusers, Washington forced his Secretary of State to resign in disgrace.

Later, when Randolph published his *Vindication* of his conduct, the President held that it merely proved his guilt:

> While at the head of my cabinet, he has been secretly, but actively, plotting with the opponents of my administration, consulting and contriving with them for the defeat of its measures; he, the Secretary of State, to whose trust the foreign relations of the country are confided, has been conducting an intrigue with the ambassador of a foreign government to promote the designs of that government, which were to overthrow the administration of which he, Randolph, was a trusted member. . . .

More than the experience with Jefferson, the Randolph affair convinced Washington that he had to abandon the seemingly unworkable ideal of a nonpartisan Cabinet. More than once he pointed out that he would not knowingly appoint another Secretary of State "whose political tenets are adverse to the measures which the *general* government are pursuing; for this, in my opinion, would be a sort of political Suicide; that it would embarrass its movements is most certain."

There was no doubt about the political orthodoxy of Washington's third Secretary of State, Timothy Pickering. He was an impeccably stanch Federalist who wholeheartedly supported the foreign policy he was entrusted to carry out. Yet, in comparison with his predecessors, particularly Jefferson, he was ill-equipped to handle the responsibilities of his new post. Admitting his deficiencies, Pickering remarked in later years that "my life had been spent in business, not in study; the office required knowledge and abilities which I did not possess."

Following the disillusioning experience with his first two Secretaries, Washington had set the precedent of making professional qualifications secondary to political in the selection of a Secretary of State. Since his day, no President has knowingly appointed a Secretary whose politics differed markedly from his own. It was then that the Secretaryship clearly became a political office—and one with relatively short tenure.

When he took office, John Adams retained Washington's Cabinet. Since he and Pickering were both Federalists, there was no question of the Secretary of State's political loyalty, but Pickering proved to lack personal loyalty to the President. After dismissing Pickering, Adams chose John Marshall for his second Secretary of State, a man not only loyal to him and his policies but also one with diplomatic experience. Marshall himself was especially sensitive to the question of political loyalty and later explained that "no consideration could induce me to be the Secretary of State while there was a President whose political system I believed to be at variance with my own."

Marshall's appointment, moreover, illustrates what was to become a general principle in the selection of a second Secretary of State—he is more the President's own choice than the original Secretary. In seeking a second, or even a third, Secretary of State a President usually has greater freedom of choice than in making his original appointment. He is less restricted by forces beyond his control. Once he has launched his Administration and paid his initial political debts, he can choose the man he thinks best qualified for the post, be it for political, personal, or other reasons. His criterion can be the selection of someone who has his trust and confidence. A second Secretary, therefore, usually owes his appointment directly to the President and does not often have an outside following. He tends to be more loyal to the President and more eager to carry out Presidential policy without dissent than does a first appointee.

Although modified by individual circumstances, this principle can be seen in the following appointments. James Buchanan, in selecting his second Secretary of State, Jeremiah S. Black, turned to a friend he trusted and respected, one who would remain loyal to him as he struggled with the terrible secession crisis of December, 1860. Grover Cleveland virtually ignored political and diplomatic considerations when he chose Richard Olney for his third Secretary of State. Although Olney had been his Attorney General, he was a Democrat without high status in the party or experience in foreign affairs, but one whose judgment Cleveland respected. William McKinley selected William R. Day, an old friend, for his second Secretary and John Hay, another friend and skilled diplomat, for his third. "There is no politics in it," a former President said of Hay's appointment.

Theodore Roosevelt left no doubt that he alone decided on Elihu Root, his second Secretary, and that political pressures had little to do with the appointment. "I wished Root as Secretary of State," he explained, "partly because I am extremely fond of him and prize his companionship as well as his advice, but primarily because I think in all the country he is the best man for the position and that no minister of foreign affairs in any country at this moment in any way compares with him."

Roosevelt's third Secretary of State, Robert Bacon, an old Harvard classmate who served only thirty-seven days, received the office as a token of friendship, an appointment free of political complications. "I am so glad," the President wrote to his son, "to have had nice Mr. Bob Bacon made Secretary of State before I went out."

Woodrow Wilson chose his second and third Secretaries of State, Robert Lansing and Bainbridge Colby, without emphasis on political considerations. Stanch Democrats had objected to both. One critic complained of Lansing:

> He is wholly unknown in the country except as a son-in-law of [John W.] Foster and a beneficiary of Republican favors. I suppose he is a Democrat by inheritance, but if he has ever turned his hand over to strengthen the party I never heard of it, and if all Democrats were of his type, Taft instead of Wilson would be President. His appointment will add no strength to the administration or the party.

Lansing had acquired experience in the State Department and was trained in international law, but Colby had neither training nor experience in matters of diplomacy. Wilson felt that Colby, a former Republican who had joined the Democratic Party in 1916 and had campaigned vigorously for him, was a man he could trust, one who was devoted to his policies and to himself. Angry Democratic politicians believed that the elevation of a former Republican to the first place in the Cabinet was a blunder destructive to party morale in Congress. "He was a decided Democrat," one of them remarked, "but he only decided lately." Colby, it seemed, lacked what politicians value most—party loyalty.

When Calvin Coolidge picked Frank B. Kellogg for his second Secretary of State, there was great surprise, for except for Charles E. Hughes, Coolidge apparently did not consult his Cabinet officers or leading Republican politicians. Personal considerations, more than other factors, seem to have motivated the appointment. Kellogg, a friend, had been notably gracious to Coolidge when, as Vice-President, the taciturn New Englander had presided over the Senate and had been snubbed or ignored by other Senators. Coolidge, it has been asserted, repaid Kellogg's kindness with the Secretaryship. Nonetheless, Kellogg was a politician and had had diplomatic experience.

Edward R. Stettinius, Jr., Franklin D. Roosevelt's second Secretary of State, was essentially a businessman with only limited experience in diplomacy and politics. The vital factor in his appointment was not politics but his unquestioning devotion to the President—a quality he had shown while serving as Under Secretary.

George C. Marshall, the second Secretary appointed by Harry S. Truman, not only had no political record, but had never voted. Both Democrats and Republicans respected him as a nonpolitical Secretary, a status that Marshall himself stressed. "I'm assuming that the office of Secretary of State, at least under present conditions, is nonpolitical," he said when he took office, "and I will govern myself accordingly."

Marshall was thus remarkably well qualified to administer Truman's bipartisan foreign policy, a policy that needed Republican support for its execution. In this sense, in his ability to work with a Republican Congress, Marshall was a political asset to the Truman Administration. Nonetheless, the fact that Truman trusted and admired him was the most important factor in his appointment.

The third Secretary of State Truman appointed, Dean G. Acheson, was a loyal Democrat whom party leaders had supported for the post, but he was not a professional politician and had never held elective office. The decisive reason for his selection was his thorough knowledge of State Department organization and broad experience in shaping foreign policy. Truman, therefore, chose Acheson because by experience and technical knowledge he was qualified for the position. "There were few men who came to the Secretaryship as fully prepared for the job and as eminently qualified as Acheson was," Truman pointed out.

President Eisenhower's second Secretary of State, Christian A. Herter, though a successful politician who had held elective office, was also a man who had a lifelong concern with foreign affairs. In his youth, he had served abroad in the Foreign Service and before taking over the State Department had been Under Secretary for two years.

Acheson's and Herter's appointments appear part of a trend toward selecting Secretaries of State for their training and experience in the handling of foreign relations, toward placing greater emphasis on professional qualifications than on political considerations. Herter's predecessor, John Foster Dulles, had had broad international experience, both as a lawyer and a diplomat; he was not an office-holding politician who had obtained the Secretaryship only as a reward for political services. No available Republican seemed better qualified by training and experience for the post, and none had worked so long to obtain it. A reporter wrote that "Dulles was trained for diplomacy as Nijinsky was for ballet." President Eisenhower once told friends, "Foster has been studying to be Secretary of State since he was five years old."

The President's statement was true at least superficially. Dulles had had a lifelong association with the Secretaryship and diplomacy, and the attainment of the office marked the culmination of an old ambition. His grandfather was John W. Foster and Robert Lansing was his uncle. "I don't suppose," he told State Department employees shortly after taking office, "that there is any family in the United States which has been for so long identified with the Foreign Service and the State Department as my family."

Yet, as Dulles himself knew, Eisenhower, like most Presidents-elect, had given weighty consideration to political factors in selecting his Secretary of State. He had chosen Dulles, as he had other department heads, partly to conciliate factions within a divided party. Although Dulles had long been associated with the Eastern wing of the Republican Party, headed by Thomas E. Dewey, of New York, he also had connections with the midwestern wing, headed by Robert A. Taft, of Ohio. A major factor in his selection seems to have been that he had managed to remain on good terms with the leaders of both groups. Dewey and Taft had urged Dulles' appointment on the grounds that he was the one Republican who could take over the State Department without creating difficulties in the transition from a Democratic to a Republican regime, without aggravating dissension in Republican ranks, and with the hope of promoting Republican unity on foreign policy.

I.

The appointment of even so fully qualified a Secretary of State as Dulles thus conformed, in part at least, to an old principle that had grown out of experience. In making their first appointments, Presidents have usually sought to use the Secretaryship to build up and strengthen their own political positions rather than to place the conduct of foreign relations in capable and experienced hands. The filling of that office, the most coveted political plum, has also followed a pattern in the over-all composition of Cabinets, one by which Presidents strive to gain broad support by balancing geographic sections and political factions.

A variation of this principle is the bargaining for Cabinet posts in pre-election deals. In addition to honoring commitments made in his behalf by his supporters, a new President frequently has to recognize strong unsuccessful rivals even though no deals were made with them. Accordingly, tradition often reserves the Secretaryship of State as the prize to be bestowed on the man to whom the President is most indebted for his election, as a consolation for his outstanding rival for the nomination, or at least as a reward for a powerful party leader.

An early example of this principle, one that included most of the main elements, was Henry Clay's appointment to the Secretaryship. That appointment also shows that even a President as experienced in foreign affairs as John Quincy Adams could not ignore the pressures of domestic politics in seeking a Secretary of State. Nor could he escape the political consequences of his act, for the selection of Clay touched off one of the bitterest feuds in the nation's history.

When the election of 1824 was cast into the House of Representatives, Clay, himself a candidate, threw his support to John Quincy Adams instead of to Andrew Jackson, contrary to his instructions from the Kentucky legislature. When, as a result, Adams became President and appointed Clay to the highest office in his power to bestow, Jackson's followers were convinced that the two men were carrying out a plot that used the Secretaryship as the reward for Clay's action. Since they believed that this had deprived Jackson of the victory he merited, they immediately cried "Bargain and corruption," and kept it up for four years.

While undoubtedly there was some kind of a political bargain involved in Clay's appointment, there was no evidence of corruption. Adams maintained that he had given Clay the Secretaryship because the Kentuckian had been a prominent candidate for President, with a large Western following, and because he was qualified for the post. In effect, Adams said he had to recognize the new importance of the West in national politics and that Clay deserved a consolation prize. Privately, he admitted that he had offered the Secretaryship to Clay as a political reward.

Being a minority President, Adams had sought in fact to unite his political opponents and friends behind him and his party. Although seemingly sinister at the time, and the result of unprecedented pressures, the appointment of a prominent rival to head the Cabinet in payment of a political debt was to become a part of the American political tradition. In appointing Clay, however, Adams did more than any of his predecessors in setting that tradition.

Even Abraham Lincoln, who, on becoming President, faced the greatest crisis in American history, would not depart from this tradition. In constructing his Cabinet, he gave representation, on the basis of geography, to powerful groups within the new Republican Party. In the battle for his nomination, moreover, his managers had bartered Cabinet posts for convention support.

Although Lincoln himself denied making any bargains, he seems to have recognized his managers' commitments as binding by offering the ranking Cabinet post to his outstanding rival for the nomination, William H. Seward, a powerful politician from New York. Lincoln realized that his own debt for Seward's support in the election coupled with Seward's leadership of the Republican Party made him the outstanding candidate for the

Secretaryship. Another prominent Republican believed that Lincoln was "under moral, or at least party, duress, to tender to
Mr. S[eward] the *first* place in the Cabinet," for if he did not
"that would excite bad feeling, and lead to a dangerous if not
fatal rupture of the party."

Seward's experience with foreign policy was limited to one year
on the Senate Foreign Relations Committee. Lincoln's reasons
for appointing him, obviously, were purely political. He needed
the support and national prestige that Seward could bring to his
Administration. In offering the post, the President-elect said that
"It has been my purpose from the day of the nomination at
Chicago to assign you, by your leave, this place in the administration." For Lincoln, foreign relations were dwarfed by the
pressing domestic crisis. He wanted and needed a political
adviser, not a foreign minister.

Thirty-six years later, William McKinley, virtually ignoring
the effect of his action on the nation's foreign relations, went
beyond Lincoln and, to pay off a political debt, juggled the
Secretaryship as if it were a sinecure. No one had done more to
guide McKinley into the White House than had Mark Hanna,
a wealthy industrialist and politician from Ohio, and no one,
in McKinley's view, more richly deserved the highest reward he
could bestow. Hanna, however, did not desire the Secretaryship
of State or any other Cabinet post. He coveted a seat as one of
the Senators from his own state, but the next election was two
years off. The only way Hanna could satisfy his desire immediately was if one of Ohio's Senators were to resign, and the
Governor appointed him to fill the unexpired term.

To reward Hanna, therefore, McKinley made a bargain with
Ohio's senior Senator, seventy-four-year-old John Sherman. If
Sherman would resign his place in the Senate so that Hanna
could take it, Sherman would be given the Secretaryship of State.
Since Sherman had a strong sense of party loyalty, saw the
Secretaryship as a post of honor and prestige that would serve as
a fitting capstone to a long and distinguished public career, and
was himself indebted to Hanna for political favors—particularly

in his tight and costly campaign for the Senate in 1892—he agreed to the scheme.

Early in January, 1897, after Sherman had resigned from the Senate, knowledge of the bargain leaked to the press and led to sharp attacks on both McKinley and Hanna. Friends urged Sherman to back out of his commitment and critics charged that the plan to kick Sherman upstairs to pay off Hanna was a sordid deal that would injure the nation's foreign relations. Sherman, the critics insisted, was not fit to take over the heavy responsibilities of the Secretaryship, especiallly when relations with Spain were in crisis. Even though Sherman had the experience of ten years on the Foreign Relations Committee of the Senate, he was, they pointed out, senile, failing mentally and physically, and plagued by loss of memory.

To Henry Adams, whose main interest at this time was in foreign affairs, "the man in the State Department seemed more important than the man in the White House." He wrote of his shock on learning of the bargain between McKinley and Sherman:

> Grant himself had done nothing that seemed so bad as this to one who had lived long enough to distinguish between the ways of presidential jobbery, if not between the jobs. John Sherman, otherwise admirably fitted for the place . . . was notoriously feeble and quite senile, so that the intrigue seemed to Adams the betrayal of an old friend as well as of the State Department. One might have shrugged one's shoulders had the President named Mr. Hanna his Secretary of State, for Mr. Hanna was a man of force if not of experience, and selections much worse than this had often turned out well enough; but John Sherman must inevitably and tragically break down.

Even though aware that Sherman was too old and not fit to hold the Secretaryship, McKinley resented the slurs on Sherman's competence and the attacks on himself for his selection. In a letter to the Editor of the *Chicago Tribune* in February, 1897, the President-elect declared that "the stories regarding

Senator Sherman's 'mental decay' are without foundation and the cheap inventions of sensational writers or other evil-disposed or mistaken people. When I saw him last, I was convinced both of his perfect health, physically and mentally, and that his prospects of life were remarkably good."

Despite the criticism, McKinley and Sherman carried out their parts of the bargain. Mark Hanna thus received his seat in the Senate, and the President obtained an incompetent Secretary of State. As the critics had prophesied, Sherman could not handle the responsibilities of his office and a year later had to resign. Privately, Sherman was bitter, saying he had accepted the Secretaryship at McKinley's urging "with some reluctance and largely to promote the wishes of Mark Hanna. The result was that I lost the position both of senator and secretary."

Fifteen years later, critics attacked Woodrow Wilson as vigorously as they had McKinley for offering the Secretaryship of State to William Jennings Bryan, a politician from Nebraska and several times the Democratic candidate for the Presidency. Bryan's selection in fact has often been cited as the classic example of how Presidents have prostituted the Secretaryship to the exigencies of domestic politics. What particularly disturbed critics was that Wilson, a lifelong student of American government, understood as have few Presidents the theoretical qualifications for the Secretaryship; yet he had selected a man with no background or experience in foreign affairs, or even in government administration. Bryan, moreover, not only lacked understanding of international relations but also had never shown more than a casual interest in foreign affairs except as a political issue at the end of the Spanish-American War.

However, the reasons for Bryan's appointment fit into the political tradition of the Secretaryship. Wilson was not, as some have suggested, indebted to Bryan for his nomination, but he was grateful to the Nebraskan for support during the election campaign, and although Wilson had succeeded him as the leader of the Democratic Party, Bryan still had a large and devoted following, probably the largest within the party. From the beginning of his fight for the Presidency, therefore, Wilson knew that if elected, he could hardly avoid offering Bryan a high post. He even declared that "if Mr. Bryan does not take a place in the Cabinet the whole country must be told the reason why."

Wilson did not really want Bryan as his Secretary of State, for he considered the Nebraskan a dangerous demagogue. At one time Wilson had said that it was a pity "that a man with his power of leadership should have no mental rudder," but Bryan's strength within the Democratic Party was too great to be ignored. He could, at the head of the Cabinet, bring broad support and political prestige to the Administration.

Bryan himself exerted no pressure on Wilson for the Secretary-ship. In an editorial in his newspaper, the *Commoner*, he even suggested that "Cabinet positions ought not to be regarded as currency with which to pay debts. The Presidents must look to the future and not to the past. We venture to hope that Governor Wilson will be governed by higher motives than gratitude in the selection of his official household."

Bryan's friends, however, were active in his behalf. Wilson, therefore, acting on the basis of political expediency, offered Bryan the Secretaryship of State "in order to have him at Washington and in harmony with the administration, rather than outside and possibly in a critical attitude." Mr. Dooley, the Irish wit, paraphrased this to say, "I'd rather have him close to me bosom thin on me back."

Although politically wise, Wilson's choice was unpopular with all except Bryan Democrats. "With all his abilities and possi-bilities," a New York newspaper said, "the Hon. William J. Bryan is about as well fitted to be Secretary of State as a cherub is to skate or a merman to play football. The intellectual make-up of the distinguished Democrat ends where the special faculties required for that particular post of usefulness and responsibility begin."

Few, if any, appointments to the Secretaryship were as ridi-culed as was Bryan's, but Wilson turned aside the criticism. "How contemptible," he wrote to Bryan in February, 1913, "the efforts of the papers are, the last few days, to make trouble for us and between us—and how delightful it is—to me, as I hope it is to you—to know, all the while, how perfect an understanding exists between us! It has been to me, since I saw you, a constant source of strength and confidence." This assurance won Bryan's devotion.

With Bryan's cooperation, Wilson could establish party harmony and concentrate on needed domestic reforms. Those reforms were of foremost concern to both Wilson and Bryan, for when Bryan became Secretary of State, foreign affairs were not critical. Bryan himself, moreover, apparently looked upon his new post as being more important for its political influence than its management of foreign relations. Despite this emphasis on domestic matters, and the barbs directed against it, Bryan's appointment did no violence to the tradition of selecting Secretaries of State. Wilson's choice and his motive were no worse than those of many of his predecessors. Bryan, moreover, turned out to be a better Secretary than might have been expected.

II.

Thomas Jefferson, the earliest Presidential predecessor to whom Wilson's own party could lay claim, chose an old friend, James Madison, for his Secretary of State. Although inexperienced in diplomacy, Madison had demonstrated outstanding ability in politics, but, most important, his political principles fitted Jefferson's. In turn, when Madison became President, he selected his two Secretaries of State primarily for domestic reasons. Like Wilson, in fact, he catered to political expediency and appointed a man he did not want.

When Madison won the Presidency he wished to transfer Albert Gallatin, who had been his Cabinet colleague under Jefferson, from the Treasury to the State Department. When the Senate got wind of the plan, a hard-core opposition to Gallatin, a Swiss by birth, immediately formed. His political enemies alleged that it would be dangerous to entrust the nation's foreign relations to a foreigner.

A key figure in the opposition was General Samuel Smith, a Senator from Maryland and the brother of Robert Smith, Jefferson's Secretary of the Navy. The Senator sought a high post, the Secretaryship of State if possible, for his brother. Fearing a split in his party at the very start of his Administration, Madison appeased General Smith and other opponents in the Senate by appointing Robert Smith, a man he did not truly trust, Secretary of State.

Smith's appointment is unique—the only instance in which the Senate was able to impose a Secretary of State on a President. Most senators recognize the need for mutual trust and confidence between the President and his Secretary of State, and hence usually give quick approval to the President's nomination.

Madison was never happy with Smith, whose appointment he insisted had grown out of a "miserable intrigue," and finally got rid of him. Smith's removal alienated powerful factions within Madison's own party whose backing his Administration needed. To compensate for this loss of support, in Virginia at least, he offered the Secretaryship to James Monroe, who earlier had fallen out with him but who had remained a powerful force in the politics of the Old Dominion. Thus Monroe, a man with extensive if not always successful diplomatic experience, gained the Secretaryship because of the political support he could bring to the President, and not for his broad professional qualifications.

Even John Quincy Adams, the next Secretary, was selected mainly on the basis of domestic political considerations. Galled by the charge that his two immediate predecessors had chosen men from Virginia to perpetuate what came to be known as the Virginia dynasty in the Secretaryship and the Presidency, James Monroe was determined not to appoint another Virginian, or even a Southerner, as Secretary of State. To avoid making his Administration appear a sectional one, resting primarily on support from south of the Potomac, he decided to placate Northern discontent and to appoint a Secretary from the Northeast.

Of the available candidates, John Quincy Adams of Massachusetts fitted best the conditions Monroe had set. "I have
thought it advisable," Monroe confided to Jefferson, "to select a
person for the dept. of State from Eastern States, in consequence
of which my attention has been turned to Mr. Adams, who by
his age, long experience in our foreign affairs, and adoption into
the republican party, seems to have superior pretensions to any
there."

True enough; no man in the country was better qualified for
the Secretaryship on the basis of diplomatic experience and
training than Adams. His introduction to the ways of diplomacy
had begun at age eleven at the knee of his father in Paris. At
fourteen, he had accompanied the American Minister to Russia
to St. Petersburg as private secretary. After that, he had held
several diplomatic posts in the capitals of Europe and had helped
negotiate the peace treaty that ended the War of 1812.

Despite Adams' outstanding diplomatic record, it must be
remembered that Monroe would surely have passed him by if he
had come from another region or if another New Englander had
had stronger political, though weaker professional, claims to the
office. As it was, Henry Clay, furious because he did not get the
post, criticized Adams' selection on the ground that the former
New England Federalist was not a true Republican.

A few years later, Andrew Jackson, who ignored diplomatic
experience, contributed more than had Madison, Monroe, or any
other President to the tradition of making political leadership
the basis for the selection of a Secretary of State. After Jackson's
time, it became relatively rare for a Secretary to have professional qualifications. Jackson offered the Secretaryship to Martin
Van Buren, a politician from New York, a man he hardly knew,
as the choice reward for political services. "I called him to the
Department of State," Jackson said publicly, "influenced by the
general wish and expectation of the republican party throughout
the Union."

Jackson's next Secretary, Edward Livingston, a friend of Van
Buren, was also strictly a political appointee, as was the next one,

Louis McLane. Old Hickory's last Secretary of State, John Forsyth, who retained the office under Van Buren, received it as a reward for supporting Jackson in his fight against the second Bank of the United States.

Other Secretaries of State before Wilson's time who had been selected mainly to pay political debts, bring support to the Administration, or merely to placate some section of the country or party, were Daniel Webster, James Buchanan, John M. Clayton, Edward Everett, William L. Marcy, Lewis Cass, James G. Blaine, Frederick T. Frelinghuysen, and Thomas F. Bayard.

A unique case is that of John C. Calhoun. A close friend and adviser of President John Tyler, who owed Calhoun a debt of gratitude, in effect offered the South Carolinian the Secretaryship of State without consulting Tyler beforehand. Although Tyler had serious misgivings about having Calhoun at the head of his Cabinet and was angered by the action of his friend, he decided against repudiating the indirect offer. To fail to nominate Calhoun after Calhoun and his friends had come to believe that he had been offered the Secretaryship would have created more enemies for an Administration that already had too many. Furthermore, Tyler lacked support from either Democrats or Whigs, and hence most prominent politicians, because they were concerned about their future, would not accept the office from him, particularly in the twilight of his Administration. Only Calhoun among the men of national stature was willing to take the post; he had already seen his greatest days; he had no political future.

Another President who appointed a Secretary of State he did not truly want because of political pressures was James K. Polk. In 1844, James Buchanan was a favorite son of Pennsylvania's Democrats, and when Polk won the Presidency, they expected to see their favorite rewarded handsomely. Pennsylvania's electors, in fact, went so far as to recommend Buchanan for the Secretaryship. Although Polk distrusted Buchanan, he could not ignore the claims of the powerful Pennsylvania party. Ironically, when Buchanan himself became President he was forced to place Lewis Cass of Michigan, a man he did not like, at the head of his

Cabinet because the Democrats of the Old Northwest demanded such recognition.

Similarly, Benjamin Harrison did not want James G. Blaine, the uncrowned king of the Republican Party, as his Secretary of State, but Blaine's supporters expected him to be paid off generously for his contributions to Harrison's campaign. A large majority of the leading Republicans, and almost without exception the rank and file of the party, expected him to be given the Secretaryship.

"The whole country knows," a friend told Harrison, "that the first great question before your mind in preparing the programme for your administration is as to the form in which you shall give consideration to the formidable personality of Mr. Blaine." Discerningly, he advised the President-elect to offer Blaine the Secretaryship, saying, "I should fear it would be accepted as a confession of self-distrust if you do not invite him." Finally, without overcoming his misgivings, Harrison offered Blaine the post, saying he did so to preserve party harmony and "to avoid anything that would promote dissensions."

III.

Presidents by accident, that is, those who have succeeded to their office through the Vice-Presidency—Tyler, Andrew Johnson, Chester A. Arthur, Theodore Roosevelt, Coolidge, and Truman —were also concerned about party harmony and hence frequently kept their predecessors' Secretaries of State. They wished to give the impression of carrying on the dead President's policies and hence hoped to inherit his political support.

Sometimes, as in the case of Millard Fillmore's appointment of Daniel Webster to the Secretaryship and even in Truman's replacement of Edward R. Stettinius, Jr., with James F. Byrnes, the accidental Presidents have acted on the principle that to escape the dead grip of their immediate predecessors, they must have a Secretary of their own choice. Incidentally, this principle can be stretched to cover most cases of a President succeeded by

another of his own party. Only two elected Presidents, John
Adams and Martin Van Buren, have continued with the Secretaries of State who were in office when they took over.

One President to whom political principle or tradition meant
little was Ulysses S. Grant. Elected as a military hero, without
knowledge of politics and affairs of state, he chose his Secretaries
of State without concern for professional qualifications and in
defiance of established political principles. Believing apparently
that he was not obligated to politicians, Grant picked his Secretaries to suit himself and without consulting party leaders. He
said he had appointed Elihu B. Washburne, a friend from his
home town of Galena, Illinois, as a token of gratitude for favors
and to give him prestige for a later appointment as Minister to
France. Washburne held the Secretaryship for only ten days, and
five of those were on sufferance while he awaited a successor to
relieve him.

In his search for a permanent Secretary, Grant at one time
considered John Lothrop Motley, a noted historian with diplomatic experience, but Motley's surface eccentricity doomed him.
"He parts his hair in the middle, and carries a single eyeglass!"
Grant told a friend after meeting Motley. Grant would have no
monocled foreign-looking dandy at the head of his State Department.

Rutherford B. Hayes also flouted political principle in selecting his Secretary of State. Even before he was certain of his election to the Presidency, he wrote in his diary, "I am inclined to
say, that I must not take either of the leading competitors for
the Presidential nomination, nor any member of the present
cabinet." Therefore, as a reform candidate, he appointed a leader
of the liberal faction in the Republican Party, William M.
Evarts of New York, to head his Cabinet.

The regular Republicans objected. One of the New York
bosses told Hayes that "the working Republicans of the State
would not have supported a man who had never shown his faith
by his works, who had received wealth and honor from an Administration [Grant's] he has publicly abused and vilified, and

whose record as a Republican has been more than doubtful." Hayes, the regulars believed, was defying the leadership of the party. Some of them even tried to organize a revolt against him and to kill Evarts' appointment in the Senate, but this failed.

Democrats raised similar objections in 1892, when Grover Cleveland, with no need to use the Secretaryship of State as a consolation prize to conciliate a prominent rival, offered it to Walter Q. Gresham, a Republican recently turned Democrat, a man without diplomatic experience. Apparently, Cleveland sought to hold in a kind of fusion the support of independents and disaffected elements of the Republican Party. "You are strong and represent a large class who have not heretofore stood with our party," he told Gresham in asking him to take the post.

Nonetheless, old Democrats and new associates alike regarded Gresham with distrust, believing that a prize as important as the Secretaryship should go to none but a highly placed regular Democrat. While recognizing that Gresham's support had contributed to Cleveland's victory, the regular Democrats believed that his contribution, though valuable, did not merit such a high reward.

Later Presidents, in most instances, followed the traditional pattern in selecting their Secretaries of State. Warren G. Harding, leaning on the advice of friends, appointed Charles E. Hughes, a nationally prominent Republican and former Presidential candidate without any background in foreign affairs, as his Secretary, an appointment that pleased most party leaders. Herbert Hoover, although solicitous about the political needs of his Administration, also showed some concern for the management of foreign relations. He finally selected Henry L. Stimson, a lawyer from New York, for his Secretary, because he appeared to be the only prominent Republican available who had some knowledge of foreign affairs.

To serve his domestic political needs, Franklin D. Roosevelt chose Cordell Hull, who had some Congressional background in foreign affairs but no experience in diplomacy, for his Secretary of State. Coming to the Presidency in a time of great internal crisis, Roosevelt knew he would need strong Congressional support to carry out a recovery program. In several particulars, Hull was an ideal candidate for liaison between the White House and Capitol Hill. Having served many years in both House and Senate and having been Chairman of the Democratic National Committee, Hull carried considerable prestige with the men who composed the Democratic majorities. They knew and respected him, and Southerners venerated him as their most distinguished representative in government. No President in Roosevelt's position, particularly one with his political sagacity, could overlook the assets Hull could bring to his Administration.

Hull's record, moreover, was good. In 1932, he was one of the first to jump on the Roosevelt bandwagon and had used his considerable influence among Southern party leaders to gain support for Roosevelt's nomination. He was one of the small group of preconvention Roosevelt supporters who believed that with victory they would be rewarded with high offices. From the outset, therefore, in recognition of Hull's part in the kingmaking, Roosevelt had marked him for a Cabinet post. When he finally offered the Tennessee politician the Secretaryship, he pleased old-line party leaders and assured himself the support of valuable allies in Congress.

Like Roosevelt, Harry Truman placed a Southern politician with a strong following in Congress in the Secretaryship of State —James F. Byrnes of South Carolina, a man who had also been his rival. In 1944, Byrnes had sought the Democratic nomination for Vice-President and when Truman, more acceptable to various factions within the party as a compromise candidate, received it instead, Byrnes was bitterly disappointed. "I thought," Truman wrote in explaining his appointment, "that my calling on him at this time might help balance things up." Truman also knew that Byrnes would bring far more political prestige to his Administration than could Stettinius, whom he was replacing, and would be an invaluable ally in working with the Southerners, who controlled the conservative coalition that ran Congress.

In his memoirs, Truman gives still another reason for appointing Byrnes. As the law of Presidential succession stood at the time, the Secretary of State was, in effect, also the Vice-President, and hence presented a special problem. Stettinius had never held an elective office; in fact he had never even been a candidate.

"It was my feeling," Truman wrote, "that any man who stepped into the presidency should have held at least some office to which he had been elected by a vote of the people." Truman wanted to change the law of Presidential succession so that a man who had been elected to office would replace the Secretary in the line of succession. "Pending a change in the law," he explained, "I felt it my duty to choose without too much delay a Secretary of State with proper qualifications to succeed, if necessary, to the presidency. At this time I regarded Byrnes as the man best qualified."

Thus, regardless of the variation in the pattern of selection, concern for the handling of foreign relations has seldom been foremost. Until the years of the Cold War, the Secretaryship of State had retained as one of its prominent characteristics one it had acquired in Washington's day; it was an office to be filled mainly by politicians to meet the domestic needs of the President. This need, of course, did not in theory preclude a concern for foreign policy, too, in making the appointment, but in practice it too often did.

In the years of the Cold War, when anxiety over foreign relations has become a foremost national concern, the appointment of such professionally qualified men as Acheson, Dulles, and Herter indicates that a dramatic change has taken place in the selection of Secretaries of State. Dean Rusk also can be called something of a professional, one with considerable diplomatic experience. He had served in the State Department for years in various capacities, and for a time as Deputy Under Secretary, before becoming the head of the department. When President-elect Kennedy offered him the Secretaryship, Rusk was President of the Rockefeller Foundation, a man knowledgeable in foreign affairs but without a national reputation or political following. In selecting Rusk, Kennedy passed over men like Adlai E. Stevenson and Chester Bowles, who had been rivals for the nomination, had strong political followings, and could claim experience in and knowledge of foreign affairs. The trend of selecting a Secretary of State mainly for his qualifications in the handling of foreign affairs thus appears to have become a new pattern.

4

Heir Apparent and Prime Minister

By the superior real and inherent importance of the
Department of State in the organization of this Government, and by the successive transfer of two Secretaries of State to the Presidency, a general impression
has pervaded the Union of a higher consideration due
to that Department, and that in the practice of the
Government it is the natural introduction to the head
of the Executive.

—John Quincy Adams, 1819

THE first two Vice-Presidents, John Adams and Thomas Jefferson, both succeeded to the Presidency and seemed to have
formed a precedent for Vice-Presidential succession, but Jefferson's rupture with his own Vice-President, Aaron Burr, destroyed
the pattern. Then by designating Secretary of State James Madison heir apparent, Jefferson endowed the Secretaryship with a
special political significance.

Thus, quite early in the history of the Republic, men entered
the Secretaryship of State with their eyes fixed on the future, a
future that lay only one step above them. The Secretaryship, in
other words, was coveted as the steppingstone to the White
House. Madison, James Monroe, and John Quincy Adams all rose
directly from that office to the Presidency. Since the man who
was chosen Secretary appeared to have a distinctive claim to
the Presidency, men came to desire the Secretaryship not for its
own virtues or as an end in itself, but for its political promise. So
high did the prestige of that office rise that factions within the
Jeffersonian party fought tooth and claw to control it.

Another reason for the Secretaryship's high repute was that in the early national period, foreign relations were a foremost concern in the councils of the government. Accomplishments in foreign affairs reflected glory on both the President and the Secretary of State. Most of those who held the Secretaryship, moreover, were men of exceptional ability. All these factors contributed to the status of the office as the steppingstone to the Presidency.

Sensitive to these factors, Madison's second Secretary, James Monroe, took over the Secretaryship determined to make use of it as the last step to the White House. Before accepting the offer of the office, however, he had written to two friends for advice. Both urged acceptance with almost identical arguments. The Secretaryship, they stressed, would keep him before the public and hence would offer a better opportunity to succeed to the Presidency than would his present post as Governor of Virginia. One of them advised:

> Our foreign relations seem to be drawing to a crisis, and you ought to be in the public eye when it happens, for your own sake, independently of the service you can render to your country. . . . This offer to you is an indication of a disposition in Mr. Madison to relieve himself of the burden [of foreign affairs]; and if you suffer yourself to lose the benefit of this disposition, another will gain it to your inestimable injury. Suppose this other should be a competitor for the Presidency, will it not be a decisive advantage over you?

Following this advice, Monroe accepted, became heir apparent, and succeeded to the Presidency.

Although the next Secretary, John Quincy Adams, entered the office concerned primarily with his responsibilities as a Cabinet officer and head of the Department of State, he and his friends also showed a sensitiveness to his special position in the Presidential succession. One friend told old John Adams:

> It seems to me that the office of secretary of state, the talents of the candidates being equal, is the stepladder to the presidential chair, at

least it has been so in the case of the last three presidents. Now as your son, the Honorable John Quincy Adams, is appointed to that station, if he makes the best advantage of his situation, it is more than probable that he may be the next president of the United States.

Six months later, though Monroe attempted to treat rival Presidential aspirants in his Cabinet with impartiality, rumor had it that he intended "to make his Secretary of State his eventual successor, and that he will in due time give evidence of such intentions." Such stories angered Adams' rivals, set him up as the target for politically inspired attacks, and led to assaults on the pre-eminence of the Secretary of State in the Cabinet. From the beginning of Monroe's Administration, in fact, the other department heads made it clear that they expected "an entire equality with the Secretary of State" and that they considered "as an offensive distinction in his favor" certain ceremonial priorities his office enjoyed.

"My office of Secretary of State," Adams himself complained, "makes it the interest of all the partisans of the candidates for the next Presidency (to say no more) to decry me as much as possible in the public opinion." The political influence of his office, the idea that almost by prerogative it would place him in the Presidency—and not its control of foreign relations—lay, Adams was aware, at the root of his colleagues' jealousy.

Adams' rivals were justified in fearing him, for he was ambitious and, as much as any man, wanted to become President, hoping that the Secretaryship would again lead directly to the White House. For him it did. Although not as popular as other candidates or as schooled in politics, he had the advantage of running on a record of accomplishment in foreign policy.

Despite the attacks on what the Jacksonians called the "Secretary dynasty," Adams' successor, Henry Clay, came to believe that the nation would continue to follow "safe precedents" and hence accepted the Secretaryship with the idea of using it to gain the Presidency. The circumstances of his appointment, which set the pattern for employing the Secretaryship as a consolation prize, and the public reaction to the cry "bargain and corruption," however, led to the breaking of the Secretarial succession. As Secretary of State, Clay became the main issue in John Quincy Adams' beleaguered Administration and never obtained the higher prize he so earnestly sought. Instead of clearing the path to the White House, the Secretaryship under Clay became a dead end for anyone with Presidential ambitions.

One reason for this change was Andrew Jackson's victory in 1828—a victory that marked the end of the caucus, the rise of the nominating convention, and the death of the "Secretary dynasty." Since Washington's day, every President had had experience in foreign affairs, either abroad as a diplomat or as Secretary of State. So important were foreign relations in those formative years that they had pre-empted a good part of the public life of those Presidents, but not so with Jackson. A soldier and frontier lawyer, he had had no diplomatic experience and had never held an administrative post that dealt essentially with foreign affairs. His primary interests, like those of the nation he headed, were domestic. Under him, therefore, the Secretaryship entered a new era, one that saw it descend from the heights of politics and statesmanship.

Jackson, who nurtured a deep hostility toward the "Secretary dynasty," laid down the rule that Presidential aspirants were ineligible for Cabinet appointments, meaning essentially that the Secretaryship of State henceforth would be closed to them. Since succeeding Presidents who adhered to the Jacksonian tradition adopted this principle also, the Secretaryship became in time an office that those who still aspired to the Presidency would try to avoid.

Nonetheless, Jackson's first Secretary of State, Martin Van Buren, accepted the post because, among other reasons, he believed it still might be used as a springboard to the Presidency. His appointment, he realized, symbolized the rising power of his state, New York, in national politics and the eclipse of Virginia, which had been the home of Secretaries of State as well as of Presidents. As a shrewd politician, he knew, therefore, that the

Secretaryship, despite its decline in status, retained considerable prestige.

When Van Buren resigned, he camouflaged his desire for the Presidency, however. He published a letter saying he was giving up the Secretaryship because Jackson had consented to accept a second term. Since he himself, because of the reputation of the Secretaryship but against his will, was considered the next successor to the Presidency, he could not properly remain in the Cabinet. To do so, he asserted, would draw attacks upon the Administration and its measures. He declared that he wished to set an example for the country by removing the politics of Presidential succession from the Cabinet; in fact, he left the Secretaryship for the same reason he had taken it: mainly because he thought the change would advance his political career.

Van Buren did succeed Jackson to the Presidency, but not from the Secretaryship or as a result of his work as Secretary. He did so from the Vice-Presidency.

William Henry Harrison, who won the Presidency from Van Buren, first offered the Secretaryship to Clay. Since Clay had never been happy in the State Department and knew from experience that the post was no longer the last step before the White House, he turned down the offer. Daniel Webster, however, accepted the office from Harrison, hoping it would once again open the door to the Presidency, if not immediately, perhaps later.

The next Jacksonian President, James K. Polk, like Jackson himself, wished to exclude Presidential hopefuls from the Cabinet but, for political reasons, violated this rule by appointing James Buchanan, a known aspirant, as Secretary of State. Polk, however, tried to protect himself against Buchanan's ambition by pledging him, as he did other Cabinet officers, to resign immediately if he were to become an active candidate for the Presidency.

Buchanan's acceptance of the Secretaryship, however, was so qualified that, in effect, he managed to evade Polk's conditions. While stating that "both patriotism & policy—the success of the party, as well as that of your administration, require that we should have repose from the strife of making Presidents," he also told Polk he "could and would not accept the high and honorable office to which you have called me, at the expense of self-ostracism." Nonetheless, Polk took Buchanan's statement as a pledge and placed him at the head of his Cabinet.

The arrangement was never a happy one. Believing that Buchanan had begun maneuvers to succeed him almost on the day he became Secretary of State, Polk never fully trusted him. Increasingly alarmed by his Secretary's ambition, the President wrote in his diary in December, 1847:

> I regret to be under the impression that for some weeks past Mr. B. seems to have been so much absorbed with the idea of being President that I cannot rely, as formerly, upon his advice given in Cabinet upon public subjects. My impression is that all his opinions are formed and controlled by the consideration of the means best calculated to enable him to succeed in getting the nomination as my successor. He seems to have lost sight of the success of my administration & to be acting alone with a view to his own personal advancement.

Several months later, shortly before the Democratic Presidential nominating convention, Polk gained the impression that his Secretary of State was guilty of treachery and weighed the idea of dismissing him. Friends had told Polk that Buchanan, fearing that Polk would run for a second term, had engaged a newspaper writer to attack the President and thus perhaps prevent his renomination. Polk's suspicions proved unfounded, but they reveal the depth of his concern over the succession and how little faith he had in his Secretary of State.

Although unable to use the Secretaryship as the final direct step to the White House, Buchanan ultimately gained the Presidency—the last Secretary of State to do so. Political considerations not connected with the Secretaryship, however, made him the Chief Executive.

Even though by Buchanan's day the belief that the Secretary would be elevated to the Presidency was virtually dead, the memory of that tradition lingered on in the late nineteenth and well into the twentieth century. In 1880, James A. Garfield, before offering James G. Blaine the Secretaryship, asked, "Please tell me whether you are or will be the candidate for the presidency in 1884. I ask this because I do not purpose to allow myself nor any one else to use the next four years as the camping-ground for fighting the next presidential battle." Believing that he could not obtain the Presidential nomination by soliciting it and that if it were to come to him, it would come seemingly unsought, Blaine answered that he "would not again seek the nomination," and accepted the Secretaryship.

A quarter of a century later, when Theodore Roosevelt appointed Elihu Root Secretary of State, rumors circulated that Root nursed Presidential ambitions and had now become heir apparent. Specifically, that gossip told of an agreement whereby Root had accepted the Secretaryship in return for Roosevelt's promise to aid him in securing the Republican nomination in 1908, but there is no evidence of such a bargain.

Some of Root's friends who wanted him to be President feared that by taking over the Secretaryship, which they considered a dead end, he would kill his chances for the higher prize. One of them sent him a telegram asking, "Would it not be best to wait three years for the substance rather than take the shadow now?" "My feeling," Root answered, "is that the things one has the opportunity to do are substance and the things one tries to get are shadow." But Root never became President.

More than a quarter of a century later, Cordell Hull held the Secretaryship believing that Franklin D. Roosevelt had designated him heir apparent and that he would move up to the Presidency after Roosevelt's second term. When Roosevelt ran for a third term, therefore, Hull felt betrayed. Since a Gallup public-opinion poll, whatever its worth, suggested that he was more popular than the President himself, Hull blamed what he called the "extreme left fringe" and its influence over the President for shutting him out of the White House.

Within the same decade, George Marshall's appointment to the Secretaryship aroused speculation that he would be a candidate for the Presidency in 1948, but Marshall scotched such talk. That, perhaps, was the last revival of the old tradition of Secretarial succession.

In the frustrating years of the Cold War, when foreign policy aroused public passions as seldom in the past, and the Secretary of State was compelled to uphold unpopular policies, even his "availability" as a Presidential candidate, if he had the other necessary qualifications and support, was practically destroyed. Few politicians who thought they had a good chance to win the Presidency, therefore, would eagerly take the Secretaryship.

With foreign relations demanding constant attention and occupying a Secretary's full energies, moreover, he did not have time for fence-mending with local politicians—an essential activity in the making of a President. Some students of American foreign policy even argue that the new urgency of foreign affairs demands a Secretary of State whose qualifications are so specialized that they would disqualify him from consideration as a Presidential candidate.

I.

After the Jacksonians had destroyed the "Secretary dynasty," a new concept of the Secretaryship arose. If they could not step from the State Department to the White House, some Secretaries of State reasoned, perhaps they could use their office as a prime minister would and actually run the government, or at least gain broad power. Apparently, the first Secretary to take office with this idea in mind, as well as with the hope of ultimately gaining the Presidency, was Daniel Webster.

In 1841, when William Henry Harrison, a military hero of advanced years, became President, Whig leaders, reacting against the strong executive leadership of the Jackson years, envisaged an eclipse of Presidential power. Looking upon Harrison as a figurehead, Webster planned to make most of the important decisions, in effect, to run the Administration as if he were prime minister. The Whig politicians, for instance, induced Harrison to bring administrative and policy matters before the Cabinet, which they controlled, for decision by majority vote. Under this scheme, the President, like the department heads, would have only one vote. Webster, as the leader of the Cabinet, was never able to carry out his part in controlling this experiment, for Harrison's sudden death after one month in office, followed by the accession of John Tyler, something of a political maverick not controlled by Whig leaders, threatened the Secretary's premiership.

Even though Tyler asked the department heads to remain, all but Webster resigned. The Secretary of State knew, however, that he could not take the part of a prime minister, for when he told the new President of Harrison's agreement to run the government by majority decision of the Cabinet, Tyler announced that "I, as President, shall be responsible for my administration." Yet Tyler allowed his Secretary to initiate policy and accepted his ideas and guidance in foreign relations. Since Webster made the most of his broad discretionary powers and actually formulated foreign policy, his brief but brilliant tenure as Secretary, though not that of a prime minister, contributed substantially to his reputation as a statesman.

Tyler's third Secretary of State, John C. Calhoun, overshadowed the President in political stature and statesmanship. In taking office, Calhoun, too, considered himself virtually a prime minister. Later, Calhoun claimed that he had chosen the means that had brought about the immediate annexation of Texas, the outstanding accomplishment of Tyler's Presidency. Referring to the South Carolinian as the "great I am," Tyler vehemently denied his claim for credit. "*If he selected,*" Tyler said, referring to the method used in acquiring Texas, "then Texas is not legitimately a State of the Union, for Congress gave the power *to the President to select,* and not to the *Secretary of State.*"

The next two Whigs, Zachary Taylor and Millard Fillmore, were weak Presidents who took as Secretaries of State men Whig politicians expected to function as prime ministers. Taylor, like Harrison, is reputed to have been a captive of his Cabinet, and his Secretary, John M. Clayton, was at first expected to be the Administration's strong man. Clayton, however, was never able to provide the Administration with the leadership it needed.

Taking over the Presidency after Taylor's death, in July, 1850, Fillmore gave Daniel Webster a second turn in the Secretaryship. In political stature, experience, and statesmanship Webster again outshone the President, and this time, when he was not sick, he took up the part of a prime minister. Since the most pressing problems were domestic, he devoted himself mainly to this area, bringing the Administration, for instance, decisive support in the Compromise of 1850.

Jeremiah S. Black, who took over the Secretaryship as a lame duck in the middle of December, 1860, after Buchanan's Administration had been repudiated and civil war threatened, also concerned himself almost wholly with domestic affairs. Although Black held office for less than three months, he acquired great power because Buchanan, confronted with a national crisis beyond his grasp, relied on him for guidance. When, for example, Black threatened to resign because Buchanan appeared to concede too much to the seceding South, the President pleaded with him to stay, saying, "I have leaned upon you in these troubles as upon none other, and I insist that you stand by me to the end." The Secretary stayed, and in the last three weeks of the Administration, he and three colleagues formed a Cabinet regency, which made the important decisions. Buchanan was reduced almost to a nominal chief of state and his forceful Secretary of State acted virtually as a prime minister.

From the day he was invited to join the Cabinet, the next Secretary of State, William H. Seward, expected to govern as a prime minister, to direct the entire government in the President's name. Believing that he alone could head off the disaster of civil war, he wrote to his wife in December, 1860, when he received the offer, "I have advised Mr. Lincoln that I will not decline. It is inevitable. I will try to save freedom and my country."

Seward told friends that Lincoln wanted him for his "prime minister." To a foreign diplomat, he explained that "there is no great difference between an elected President of the United States and an hereditary monarch. The latter is called to the throne through the accident of birth, the former through the chances which make his election possible. The actual direction of the public belongs to the leader of the ruling party, here as well as in any hereditary principality." Seward, of course, considered himself the chieftain of the ruling Republican Party.

Public opinion, North and South, seemed to concur in Seward's estimate of his expected status as Secretary of State. Since Lincoln was an unknown quantity, many assumed that he did not have the qualities needed to grapple with the secession crisis. They concluded that he had called on Seward, a man far more experienced in government than himself, not only to handle foreign relations and head the Cabinet, but also to run the government and make the vital decisions. The Secretary of State, many believed, would be President in fact.

In the three months before Lincoln's inauguration, the relationship between the President-elect and Seward seemed to give substance to these assumptions. Lincoln sought Seward's advice and assistance in various political matters. He asked Seward to keep him informed of the state of political parties and the temper of opinion among politicians in Washington and to offer suggestions on bringing loyal Southerners into the Cabinet so as to give it a broad geographical base. The public and politicians of both major parties, therefore, had reason to look upon Seward as the spokesman for the incoming Administration.

After the inauguration, Lincoln gave his Secretary of State a relatively free hand in foreign affairs and continued to consult him on other matters, but for Seward that was not enough. Less than a month after taking office, he made a bold bid for executive power. In a paper modestly headed "Some Thoughts for the President's Consideration," he suggested diverting public attention from the crisis over slavery by centering it on foreign grievances, evoking a surge of unity and patriotism, possibly with declarations of war against France and Spain. The heart of the plan, however, was Seward's offer to take over direction of the government.

"Whatever policy we adopt," the Secretary pointed out, "there must be an energetic prosecution of it. For this purpose it must be somebody's business to pursue and direct it incessantly. Either the President must do it himself, and be all the while active in it, or devolve it on some member of the Cabinet. . . . It is not my especial province, but I neither seek to evade nor assume responsibility."

Keeping the contents of this remarkable document to himself, Lincoln tactfully put his Secretary of State in his place and refused to abandon any of his own responsibilities. "Upon your closing propositions," he told Seward, "I remark that if this must be done, I must do it."

A month later, Seward wrote home that "a country so largely relying on my poor efforts to save it has refused me the full measure of its confidence needful to that end. I am a chief reduced to a subordinate position, and surrounded by a guard, to see that I do not do too much for my country, lest some advantage may revert indirectly to my own fame."

Despite this early rebuff and the fact that the President had made it clear that he himself would exercise the ultimate control in all matters, Seward succeeded in gaining vast power and, in the conduct of foreign relations, in retaining what seemed almost unlimited freedom. In time, Lincoln came to place such trust in his Secretary of State that when Seward sent him a document for approval he signed without question or asked merely where his signature should go. In certain areas of executive authority, Lincoln allowed his Secretary to act virtually as a dictator. Seward interfered in the work of other departments, conceived military and domestic policies, and had at his disposal a secret-service organization to carry out those policies, policies that Lincoln himself seldom questioned.

Seward appeared with the President constantly and frequently visited the armies with him. Since he lived near the White House, he spent a good part of each day with Lincoln and was always ready with ideas and proposals, but his influence with the President aroused the jealousy of his Cabinet colleagues. Gideon Welles, the Secretary of the Navy, wrote that Seward "has the inside track and means to keep it" and "is anxious to direct, to be the Premier, the real Executive."

Whether or not they liked it, most members of the Cabinet accepted it as a fact that Seward, next to the President, was the Administration's guiding spirit. Welles recorded that in the infrequent early Cabinet meetings, the Secretary of State "assumed, and was allowed, as was proper, to take the lead in consultation and also to give tone and direction to the manner and mode of proceedings. The President, if he did not actually wish, readily acquiesced in this."

To the public, too, the Secretary of State appeared the dominating member of the Administration. Even Mrs. Lincoln, who hated Seward and called him "a dirty Abolitionist sneak," believed that he ran the government. "He draws you around his little finger like a skein of thread," she said to her husband.

Both the public and Mrs. Lincoln overestimated Seward's influence; he did not dominate Lincoln. After his initial efforts to control, the Secretary recognized Lincoln's finer qualities, accepted him as the true and active head of the government, and reconciled himself to his own subordinate status under the President. "It was not Mr. Lincoln who conformed himself and his policy and general views to Mr. Seward," a Cabinet member explained, "but it was Mr. Seward who adapted himself with ease and address to Mr. Lincoln, and, failing to influence, adopted and carried out the opinions and decisions of his chief."

Lincoln trusted his Secretary of State and relied on him for policy and guidance more than he did on the other department heads because he found in Seward a loyal, resourceful, and intelligent assistant, one willing to take needed risks in a time of great crisis. In his reach for power and in the power Lincoln allowed him, therefore, Seward was able to extend his grasp far beyond control of foreign affairs and to become more than a Secretary of State. He viewed and attempted to use his office as a premiership, one that functioned with Lincoln's support, to gain access to all branches of the government.

"I am counselling with the Cabinet one hour, with the Army officers the next, the Navy next, and I visit all the troops as fast as they come," the Secretary of State wrote in 1861, describing his activities. "I dare not," he added, "because I cannot safely, leave this post from which all supplies, all directions, all inquiries must radiate, to armies and navies at home and to legations abroad."

Seward tended to inflate his own importance. Yet, in his record under Lincoln can be found precedents for tremendous power in the Secretaryship.

Under Andrew Johnson, as under Lincoln, Seward exercised a constant influence on domestic as well as foreign policy. He was close to Johnson, seemingly with him at all times, had unrestricted access to him, day or night, and was ready with advice on almost any issue. Like Lincoln, Johnson grew fond of Seward, whom he called "the old Roman." He relied heavily on him for advice, accepted his ideas readily, and delegated broad power to him. Seward, therefore, became the Administration's central figure, but the President did not abdicate his own responsibilities, and he himself exercised the power of final decision.

Under both Lincoln and Johnson, Seward tried to function as would a prime minister. He even wrote his diplomatic correspondence, which he promptly released to the press, in the style of political pamphleteers; he did so with the idea of influencing public opinion, thus showing a concern for the domestic political reaction which reflected his desire to create a premiership that could not in fact exist in the American system. Yet, in the sense that he was actively the leader of the official family, the department head entrusted to carry out major policies, Seward, perhaps more than any other Secretary of State, had acted as a kind of prime minister.

In the next Administration, Hamilton Fish did not accept the Secretaryship with the idea of becoming a prime minister, but if any one person provided the Grant Administration with leadership, he did. More than was necessary for a mere ceremonial head of the Cabinet, the other department heads deferred to him and accepted his leadership. Policies attributed to Fish created more interest than those of any other government official, for the public looked upon his policies as those of the Administration. Even newspapermen, in attempting to get at the inside of the Grant Administration, went to the Secretary of State; they constantly pressed him for interviews.

It was clear that Grant leaned heavily on his Secretary of State. On almost all matters, the President carefully weighed Fish's views and often pushed aside his own to accept his Secretary's. He allowed Fish full responsibility for the conduct of foreign relations, gave him unquestioned administrative authority, and in most other areas permitted him to exert a moderating influence, often a decisive one. So essential did Fish become as a policy-maker that Grant, upset by his Secretary's frequent attempts to resign, insisted that he could spare any member of his official family except Fish. At one time, with Grant's support, the Vice-President and forty-four Senators signed a letter urging Fish not to retire.

A man of recognized ability, Fish gave character to an otherwise tawdry and scandal-plagued Administration. As a Secretary of State, he is unique in that he did not crave great power and yet shaped policies beyond those of his own department. In effect, he too functioned as a kind of prime minister.

II.

In a few instances, the Secretaries of State who strove for the status of prime ministers believed that they, not their chiefs, deserved to be President. Blaine, like Seward, was one of those. No one else, he told Garfield in accepting the Secretaryship, could bring the Administration the political support he could. He accepted the office, moreover, with the idea in mind of running the government from the State Department, of functioning like a grand vizier. This desire surprised no one, for Blaine's lust for power was as well known as the bear's appetite for honey.

"Did your going into the State Department simply mean that you were to be Secretary of State," Blaine's eldest son wrote, "I do not think any of your friends would greatly desire it. But your taking that position will mean—and the country will so understand it—that you are the head of the administration under the President, and the chief counsellor of its policy."

Although Garfield thought that Blaine deserved the Secretary-ship and wanted him to have it, this well-known desire to make policy worried him. "If you can only restrain his immense activity and keep him from meddling with the other departments," an old friend advised the President-elect, "you will have a brilliant Secretary."

As the dominant member of the Cabinet, Blaine from the first, however, refused to be restrained. He started out initiating and controlling foreign policy, and the President came to accept and approve the results. In all other matters also, Blaine offered his advice freely, in fact acted as the President's most intimate adviser, and seemingly considered himself the *de facto* head of the government. So close was he to Garfield that the Administration has been called the Garfield-Blaine administration.

Garfield's assassination, with Blaine at his side, abruptly ended the premiership. "I cannot help feeling a little blue over the loss of place," Mrs. Blaine wrote when her husband gave up the Secretaryship. "Do you suppose that a Prime Minister ever went out without a secret feeling that he was being deprived of a right?"

Eight years later, the fact that Blaine had overshadowed Garfield and held a dynamic view of the Secretaryship worried Benjamin Harrison, who reluctantly invited the "plumed knight" to a second term in the State Department. Harrison was deter-mined to be master of his own government. In his offer, there-fore, he had made it clear that he himself would make policy. Yet the public—Blaine's foes as well as his friends—expected him to dominate Harrison's Administration as he had done Garfield's. "First and foremost, James G. Blaine will be Premier of the

Harrison Administration," the *Chicago Tribune* said, "and the mugwumps can put that in their pipes and smoke it."

The newspaper pundits were wrong. Despite his experience, fame, and faithful political following, the Secretary of State could gain no power approaching that of a prime minister. Blaine was unable even to exercise a decisive control over foreign relations. The President himself shaped and controlled policy, foreign as well as domestic.

The next Secretary of State to take office thinking of himself as a prime minister was Philander C. Knox. He believed that William Howard Taft would look to him for guidance on internal as well as foreign affairs. The President did call upon him for general advice, more so than on the other department heads, but not frequently enough to please Knox, who felt that other advisers had greater influence than he.

Knox considered himself and his office important, in fact held a grandiose view of his own status. This was quite clear to those around him. "So you have noticed, too," Taft once told his military aide, "that Knox takes his office pretty seriously. I often think how Knox would enjoy playing the role of President."

Knox usually had full responsibility for the conduct of foreign relations, and the President admitted that he did. "To the record of a year's accomplishment under Secretary Knox in our foreign affairs," Taft announced to the nation, "I think I can point with pride, and yet with becoming modesty, for it is his work and not mine. All I can claim is the merit of selecting him for the task." Privately, Taft told Knox that "the comfort I have in your management of the State Department I cannot exaggerate." Nonetheless, though Knox was able to assume considerable authority on his own and was allowed more power than were most Secretaries, he was never able to become his own boss and to function as the prime minister he thought he should be.

Charles Evans Hughes, on the other hand, did not accept the Secretaryship with the idea of acting as Warren G. Harding's prime minister, but he did, in fact, become virtually his own boss. After the President-elect had named Hughes Secretary, a

choice regarded by most observers as his best Cabinet appointment, newspaper reporters asked him what his foreign policy
would be. "You must ask Mr. Hughes about that," Harding
answered. "That is going to be another policy of the next
Administration," he added, "from the beginning, the Secretary
of State will speak for the State Department."

Although pleased that he would have actual control over the
conduct of foreign relations, Hughes sought to avoid certain
other responsibilities. Concerned over her husband's chronic in-
ability to withstand political pressures, Mrs. Harding, for example, told Hughes, "You've got to help Warren resist these
demands." Hughes, however, did not envisage his position as
that of a special aide who would shield the President from political opportunists. In fact, he seldom intervened in domestic
politics.

In other matters, too, the Secretary did not grab for power.
Even though Harding, who preferred poker and drinking parties
with his cronies to the details of foreign affairs, followed Hughes's
lead in foreign policy virtually without question, Hughes did
not transform his own ideas into policy without asking beforehand for the President's approval. Furthermore, he went to the
White House practically every day to keep the President abreast
of international affairs.

Later, explaining his relations with Harding, Hughes said:

> I realized that I must take a full measure of responsibility when I
> felt definite action should be taken. I did not go to him with a state-
> ment of difficulties and ask him what should be done, but supple-
> mented my statements of the facts in particular cases by concrete
> proposals upon which he could act at once, and to which he almost
> invariably gave his approval.

A concrete example of how the Secretary exercised his control
over foreign policy can be seen in the following blunder concerning the Four-Power Pacific Treaty of 1921 with Great Britain, France, and Japan. At a regular press conference, a reporter
had asked the President if Japan's main islands were to be

included in the treaty's "guarantee" of each signatory's territory in the Pacific. "As I see it," Harding replied, "the quadrilateral treaty does not apply to Japan proper. The mainland is no more included in the provisions of the treaty than is the mainland of the United States." This view contradicted Hughes's own interpretation of the pact and created a minor crisis. Some feared that the Secretary would resign, but instead he rushed to the White House to explain the embarrassing conflict in views to Harding.

"I shouldn't have said anything about it to the press," the President confessed. "But, Hughes," he added, "when they asked me about it, I didn't want to appear to be a dub." Both then agreed that Hughes should dictate a statement correcting the error in interpretation and that the White House would issue it. In the statement Harding confessed his ignorance and retracted his original comment. To Secretary of Commerce Herbert Hoover, easygoing Harding "seemed a little afraid of his stiff Secretary of State."

Harding's successor, Calvin Coolidge, also admired Hughes, calling him the backbone of the Harding Administration and "the greatest Secretary of State this country ever had." It was not surprising therefore that Coolidge, as ignorant of foreign affairs as Harding, a man without "an international hair in his head," retained Hughes in the State Department and gave him full responsibility for the conduct of foreign relations. Coolidge seldom initiated policy and, like Harding, usually approved unquestioningly what his Secretary presented to him. He also relied on Hughes for advice on various national problems.

Without striving to become a prime minister, Hughes therefore was able to make the most of the powers inherent in the Secretaryship. In his domain of foreign affairs, particularly under Harding, he functioned as one of the nation's powerful Secretaries of State. In this sense, Hughes may be classed as one of those who exercised some of the powers of a prime minister.

Two decades later, James F. Byrnes, like Seward and Blaine before him, took over the Secretaryship believing apparently that he was better qualified for the Presidency than his chief and should have the responsibilities of a prime minister. Although Harry Truman granted him considerable independence in the conduct of foreign relations, Byrnes, seemingly disdainful of Presidential authority, desired virtual autonomy. Moreover, the ranking Democrat of the Senate Committee on Foreign Relations pointed out, "As Secretary of State, Byrnes was secretive from the start. He tried to keep things to himself as much as possible." Byrnes viewed his office and his department as comprising the policy-making agency in foreign affairs.

Byrnes's attitude bothered Truman, who became convinced that his Secretary had come "to think that his judgment was better than the President's." Truman accused his Secretary of attempting to assume the responsibilities of the President. This led to a bitter break between the two men, and to the failure of Byrnes's efforts to play the prime minister.

Unlike Truman, Eisenhower did not feel affronted by the efforts of his Secretary of State to act, in part at least, the prime minister. Disliking the daily routine of keeping up with international developments on his own, Eisenhower at the beginning of his Administration said he would obtain his information on foreign affairs from John Foster Dulles. The Secretary of State, therefore, developed closer relations with Eisenhower over a long period than did any other department head. Seemingly, when he was not traveling, he was always with the President.

Eisenhower himself said that he met more often with Dulles than with any other member of his Cabinet. Dulles alone had the freedom of the President's office, being able to enter at almost any time. When in Washington, he went to the White House every day or used his direct phone connection to the White House to call Eisenhower once or twice a day; he conferred with him and other Presidential advisers in weekly sessions of the Cabinet and the National Security Council. When abroad, Dulles telephoned or cabled reports to the President as often as every day. In other ways, too, Dulles made himself the indispensable executive officer to Eisenhower, a President seemingly eager to delegate, but not abandon, some of the arduous responsibilities of his office.

In his conferences with Dulles, the President usually chose from alternatives the Secretary presented to him. Except in emergencies, he did not shape or carry out his own foreign policy. In most instances, Dulles initiated policy and carried it out. As a result, Eisenhower's heart attack in September, 1955, which largely incapacitated him for six months did not paralyze the conduct of foreign relations. As Dulles explained, "the policies and principles" of the Administration were entirely familiar to those charged with carrying them out, and hence the President's attack did not jeopardize "the steady prosecution of our national and international policies."

Democrats complained that there was no interruption in policy because even before the heart attack the President had delegated vital responsibilities of his office to a "regency" of his personal appointees. If so, no regent appeared more powerful in his own realm than did Dulles. No Secretary of State, not even Hughes, moreover, ever appeared more completely in command of foreign policy and none was more clearly identified the world over as the maker of that policy.

With his own people, Dulles' frequent appearances on radio and television strengthened his image as the maker of policy. Those appearances, too, reflected his desire to cultivate public opinion. Most Secretaries of State leave that task to the President, but Dulles, like a prime minister, believed that foreign policy began at home and that he needed a constituency for the support of his policies.

So well known did Dulles become that he was even made the subject of a song in a New York play, a ditty so bad, it was said, that it could have been part of the Democratic National Committee's anti-Dulles campaign. Next to the President himself, Dulles was regarded as the outstanding figure in the Eisenhower Administrations, the giant of the Cabinet. People, in fact, constantly referred to the Administration's foreign policies as the Dulles policies.

True enough, most policies did originate with Dulles. Although the Secretary seems to have had virtually a blank check in the conduct of foreign relations, it should be remembered that everything he did had the President's approval and that Eisenhower was informed in advance by Dulles himself of every action taken in foreign affairs. "Foster and I," Eisenhower said, "worked, as nearly as can be imagined, as one person." Except to be a prime minister in fact, the American Secretary of State can expect no greater power.

Such power, as Dulles' Secretaryship and that of other strong Secretaries shows, must come from the President. It is not inherent in the Secretaryship. The Secretary, of course, must have ability, intelligence, and certain aggressive qualities, but without the President's need or willingness to accept a "premier," he can attain no real power on his own. This is evident in the case of Secretary Blaine, who could be virtually a prime minister under one President and something quite different under another. The American Presidential system has no place for a prime minister in the true sense of the term, but if any executive officer has approached the powers of one, it is the Secretary of State.

An important reason for this is that much more than other Cabinet officers, the Secretary of State has responsibilities that cut across departmental lines. He should be able to bring to the President analyses and points of view that integrate military, economic, social, and other factors. He, unlike the others, should be able to offer the President a synthesis that gives due weight to all relevant data, whether in or out of the field of his department. In this broad sense of having a concern for developments in all areas that may affect the national interest, the Secretary of State, if he is a strong one, certainly shares some qualities in common with a prime minister.

5

The Figurehead

The President is the only channel of communication
between this country and foreign nations, and it is
from him alone that foreign nations or their agents
are to learn what is or has been the will of the nation.
—THOMAS JEFFERSON, 1793

PRESIDENTS who have allowed their Secretaries of State minis-
terial power comprise a minority. Other Presidents, particularly in times of crisis, have taken on themselves the conduct
of foreign relations and have jealously guarded that domain
against encroachments. Even though their Secretaries might be
the true architects of foreign policy, most Presidents have usually
seen to it that any substantial success in foreign affairs was theirs,
or at least that they received credit for it.

Except for weak Presidents, or those unwilling to concern
themselves with the details of foreign affairs, direct Presidential
control of foreign policy is the rule in the American political
system. Such control, in fact, is probably the most important
single function of the Presidency, a power that the President,
even if he should so desire, can never surrender entirely to his
Secretary of State. In practice, therefore, some Presidents not
only have retained a firm grip on the conduct of foreign relations
but have also resented independent action by their Secretaries.
A few, those who have sometimes been called their own Secretaries of State, have even relegated their senior department chief
almost to the status of a figurehead.

The first President to attempt to reduce his Secretary of State practically to a figurehead was James Madison. Having spent eight years at the head of the State Department and thus being thoroughly familiar with the conduct of foreign relations, Madison as President expected to continue to keep their conduct in his own hands, leaving little more than routine administrative duties for his Secretary to perform. Moreover, when one considers the circumstances of Robert Smith's appointment to the Secretaryship and the fact that his relations with Madison while both served in Jefferson's Cabinet were not cordial, this limitation of Smith's status is not surprising.

Claiming that Smith was incompetent, Madison sometimes went so far as to write and rewrite his Secretary's official notes. He declared that the Secretary was incapable of handling the duties of his office. Whatever talents Smith may have possessed, the President said, they were not suitable to the Secretaryship of State.

Even if Smith had possessed the necessary ability, his chances for success in the Secretaryship were remote, owing partly to the ignominious status Madison gave him and partly to his own questionable conduct. Smith had been so eager to gain the Secretaryship that he accepted it knowing that he had been forced on a President who did not want him. Then after taking office, instead of trying to win the confidence of his chief, he earned further enmity by siding with Madison's enemies in the Senate. Understandably, until the President could rid himself of his unwanted Secretary, he gave him the title but not the substance of the office.

Andrew Jackson also denied his Secretaries of State real power. He took the view that a Secretary was "merely an executive agent, a subordinate," whom he could ignore if he chose. For guidance on almost all matters of policy, he relied on unofficial advisers, especially on a group known as his "Kitchen Cabinet." He even discontinued the regular meetings of the official Cabinet, thus shutting off the Secretary of State almost completely from the making of policy.

Jackson's reliance on unofficial advisers was not an innovation; nonetheless, the extensive use he gave the practice had the effect of reducing his Secretaries of State to administrative assistants, virtually to figureheads with practically no part in the shaping of foreign policy. Van Buren, of course, was an exception, yet he acquired a voice in the making of policy not because he held the Secretaryship but because he had gained admittance to the inner circle of the President's political advisers. Even though the rule that a Secretary was merely a Presidential assistant had been established before Jackson's time, it was he who anchored it deeply into the tradition of American politics.

James K. Polk, another Jacksonian who dominated the conduct of foreign relations, also lived by that rule. He wanted an administrator for his Secretary of State, one who would agree with his opinions and policies. For political reasons, however, he accepted a Secretary, James Buchanan, who frequently opposed his views. Although irritated by this opposition, Polk did not attempt to get rid of him.

"Though Mr. Buchanan differs with me on some points," Polk confided to his diary, "yet he had not in consequence of such difference embarrassed me but had shown a willingness to carry out my views instead of his, and I was desirous to retain him in the Cabinet." At another time, the President wrote of Buchanan, "He may differ with me in opinion on public questions, and when he does, having myself to bear the responsibility, I will control."

At still other times, Polk would interpret Buchanan's advice as obstructive. Once when the Secretary objected to having his views disdainfully disregarded, Polk said to himself, "Mr. Buchanan will find that I cannot be forced to act against my convictions and that if he chooses to retire, I will find no difficulty in administering the Government without his aid." Strewn throughout Polk's diary are passages equally harsh, all attesting to a strained relationship with his Secretary of State and to the President's determination to handle foreign policy as he alone saw fit.

So discouraged did Buchanan become with his menial status that in several instances he considered resigning. He never did because he feared that a break with the President would ruin his political career. Nonetheless, he did ask Polk to consult him:

> When I differ from you, it is always with reluctance and regret. I do not like to urge arguments in opposition before the whole Cabinet. I appear then to be occupying a position that is always painful to me. A little previous consultation with me on important questions of public policy relating to foreign affairs would always obviate this difficulty; because if I failed to convince you—there would then be no appearance of dissent.

Polk, however, did not allow his Secretary's views to shape his policy. Ignoring or overriding Buchanan's advice, he continued to act on his own. His brusque treatment of his Secretary, a man several years his senior, apparently opened old wounds left by the campaign of 1844, when Polk had been a "dark horse" and Buchanan a prime contender for the Presidency. Thinking himself a superior in talent and prestige, Buchanan probably found it difficult to subordinate himself and galling to be dominated, and ignominiously so, by Polk. He probably realized, too, that even outside the Administration it was known that he had no voice in policy. "Buchanan," one observer wrote, "is treated as no gentleman would treat a sensible hireling."

Thus it can be seen that if ever a President lived up to the Jacksonian principle that a Secretary of State is subordinate and should be kept so, it was Polk. He himself controlled not only the major policies, but also the details in routine matters. He would not allow his Secretary even the fiction of being responsible for foreign affairs. Under him, the Secretary functioned merely as an administrative clerk, at times almost as a lackey, a servile retainer whose main task was to carry out the President's policies regardless of his own feelings.

Buchanan's view of the Secretaryship as a burden, one he was eager to unload, is therefore, understandable. "The State Department has never been a pleasant situation for me," he wrote at the end of his term, "though it might have been so, and personally I long to enjoy the privilege of being once more a private citizen." Yet Buchanan's menial status, in part at least, grew out of his own timidity. If he had been a bolder man, a contemporary critic pointed out, the very nature of his post would have allowed him to wield more power.

Forgetting, perhaps, his own frustrating experience under Polk, Buchanan as President treated his Secretary of State as though he were a cipher. Such a Secretary, in fact, fitted Buchanan's plans. Taking the view that, with a record of important diplomatic experience and four years in the State Department, he was better qualified to conduct foreign relations than anyone he could appoint to the Secretaryship, Buchanan was from the first determined to initiate and carry out his own foreign policy. For his Secretary of State, therefore, he sought a man of national reputation who could head his Cabinet, give his Administration a respectable front, and accept the part of a figurehead gracefully. Although Buchanan was virtually compelled by domestic political considerations to offer the Secretaryship to Lewis Cass of Michigan, whom he had never liked and did not want, Cass in most respects met his requirements.

Cass, by then seventy-five, had lost his fire, but he still had awesome stature within the Democratic Party, based on a long and distinguished career in public life, and could bring prestige to the Administration, prestige that Buchanan sorely needed. At his advanced years, moreover, Cass no longer had high political ambitions and hence could offer no threat to Buchanan and the Presidency.

Before offering Cass the Secretaryship, nonetheless, Buchanan had tried to make sure that the old man would not take the office with independent ideas on the conduct of foreign relations. Using an intermediary, he asked Cass if he would accept an appointment hemmed in with restrictions. In effect, he told Cass that he could have the Secretaryship in name only, the title and honor but no real power, and that he would have to accept constant supervision. Cass agreed to Buchanan's conditions, because as a lame-duck Senator who had been defeated in 1856, he did not wish to return to Detroit a repudiated statesman. Doubtless, he also liked the idea of spending his last days in Washington holding the highest appointive office in the land—a fitting climax to his long career of public service.

The Secretaryship, however, brought Cass almost nothing but humiliation. To guide Cass's unsteady hand, Buchanan had appointed an old friend, John Appleton of Maine, Assistant Secretary of State. Working with the President, frequently independently of Cass, Appleton actually ran the Department of State. In other ways, too, whenever he could, Buchanan shunted aside his Secretary. Thus, Lord Clarendon wrote to Buchanan shortly after he took office: "I don't suppose there are many instances of the President of the United States & the English Foreign Secretary corresponding directly with each other, but if the practice is as agreeable to you as it is to me, I shall hope for its continuance."

As a result of his figurehead status, Cass had few responsibilities and accepted slights from the President that other men would have resented. In a short while, however, he apparently came to realize not only that he was excluded from the Administration's ruling inner circle but also that he had perhaps gained an empty honor at the cost of self-respect. That he was a mere figurehead had become common knowledge. "I think," Cass's predecessor wrote of him, "he begins to feel what others clearly see, that his condition is not what it ought to be or what he is bound to make it if he intends to sustain his reputation with the country."

The Secretary was incompetent, Buchanan charged, and therefore deserved to be treated as a cipher. Most of the dispatches that bear Cass's name, he explained after Cass had resigned, were written by himself, the Assistant Secretary of State, or the Attorney General:

His original drafts were generally so prolix & so little to the point that they had to be written over again entirely, or so little was suffered to remain as to make them new Despatches. All this was done with so much delicacy & tenderness that, to the extent of my knowledge, General Cass always cheerfully & even gratefully assented. So timid was he & so little confidence has he in himself, that it was difficult for him to arrive at any decision of the least consequence. He brought many questions to me which he ought to have decided himself.

Buchanan was probably unduly caustic in his estimate of Cass. Since the President himself made most of the decisions, even the minor ones, Cass, even if he had been capable, did not have the opportunity to acquire any real power in the making of decisions. Only to very few who have held the Secretaryship does the term figurehead apply so aptly as it does to Cass.

I.

Although never a figurehead in the sense that Cass was, James G. Blaine functioned as little more than an administrative subordinate under Benjamin Harrison. He took orders from a President who jealously guarded his prerogatives, one who did not relinquish power or delegate authority easily. Aware that foreign relations was the field wherein a President could most likely build a lasting reputation, Harrison was determined that he, not his Secretary, would initiate and control foreign policy.

In foreign affairs, as in other major areas, Harrison studied important questions thoroughly and perused all pertinent documents. "I found the President here going over the Samoan despatches with your Father," Mrs. Blaine wrote, in a revealing letter to one of her sons. "He sat all crumpled up, his nose and his boots and his gloves almost meeting, but he was examining those despatches with care and great intelligence, and although I am not drawn to him, I cannot refuse him the homage of respect." So closely, in fact, did Harrison supervise the State Department that it was not unusual for him to know more of what was happening there than did the Secretary of State.

"My plan," Harrison explained, "was to give each of the Departments a stated day when the Secy would come with his papers and a full consultation would be had as to appointments and as to important matters of business." And, he added, "All matters of large concern were brought to my attention, and were settled in the conference I have referred to, or in the Cabinet meeting." Blaine, as a result, did not have full control of his own department.

When an important state paper was to be drawn up, the President usually discussed it with Blaine beforehand; sometimes he even prepared an outline for the Secretary to follow. He inspected papers drafted by Blaine, revised them, and at times discarded them for new ones he himself wrote.

Blaine chafed under such close supervision. His warm and affable personality rebelled against the President's cold and impersonal attitude. Precipitate and enthusiastic about his own ideas, Blaine never felt comfortable with the restrained and intellectual President. "Harrison," Mrs. Blaine said, "is of such a nature that you do not feel at all at liberty to enjoy yourself." Being older and better known than Harrison, moreover, the Secretary found it difficult to take orders from a younger man, particularly one who was not notably gracious in his assertion of authority and who wanted it understood that he had the whip hand. To Mrs. Blaine, it was almost unbearable to see Harrison, whom she considered a political novice and referred to as that "Indiana accident," ordering her husband to do his bidding.

The President, on his part, could not help resenting his Secretary's fame and continuing leadership in the Republican Party, of which he, Harrison, was titular head. Neither he nor Blaine, as a result, was happy with their relationship. Blaine, moreover, was never able to gain the President's confidence and, except for official functions, was usually excluded from Harrison's social affairs.

Since Blaine never had a decisive voice in the shaping of foreign policy, his status could hardly rise above that of a high-ranking administrative official.

The position of John Sherman, the next Secretary of State who had no control over his own department, resembled that of Cass more than it did Blaine's. Like Cass, Sherman was old and had accepted the Secretaryship under questionable circumstances.

Knowing that the senile Sherman could not handle foreign relations effectively, McKinley expected to use him merely as a respectable figurehead. As such, Sherman had value, for despite his acquiescence in Hanna's machinations, he still retained a national reputation, still had a political following, and could still bring some prestige to the Administration.

McKinley himself controlled the conduct of foreign relations, initiating important policies and even carrying on negotiations without Sherman's knowledge. His decisions, made without his Secretary's advice, were carried out by capable subordinates within the Department of State who frequently acted independently of Sherman.

In particular, the President relied on William R. Day, a close friend from his home town whom he had appointed First Assistant Secretary of State. Day, acting as the *de facto* Secretary of State, ran the State Department. Sherman often did little more than sign the papers that Day or other assistants brought to him for formal approval. Day, for instance, had charge of the negotiations leading to the annexation of Hawaii. The Secretary of State was called upon for consultation only when the treaty was ready for his signature. Sherman thus had practically no influence on policy or on the administration of his own department.

Finally, the crisis over Cuba placed such heavy demands on the State Department that Sherman could not carry even his limited responsibilities. Day took over virtually all his duties and, contrary to the usual practice, began to attend Cabinet meetings. Frustrated by his own inadequacies and humiliated by the fact that Day now openly represented his department in front of the other department heads, Sherman resigned immediately after the outbreak of the war with Spain.

A contemporary wrote:

> Poor Sherman makes everyone connected with the Department apprehensive. As Assistant Secretary of State, William R. Day has proved as great a diplomat in handling the situation within the Department as the International situation without. Upon Day has fallen everything of trouble from within and without. He has been compelled to

watch the venerable Secretary and guard the country from mistakes. The great career of John Sherman should have closed in some other way.

Sherman, obviously, served as Secretary of State in name only. For him the Secretaryship was a sad and inglorious twilight.

McKinley's next Secretary, John Hay, who continued in office under Theodore Roosevelt, is considered one of the outstanding Secretaries of State. His friend Henry Adams claimed that Hay was "the most imposing figure ever known in the office. He had an influence that no other Secretary of State ever possessed . . . and he stood far above counsel or advice." Hay's work under McKinley offered some basis for this extravagant estimate, for the President allowed him to shape some of his own ideas into policy. Under McKinley, therefore, Hay had a noteworthy part in formulating foreign policy, but under Roosevelt his status changed.

The relationship between Hay and Roosevelt, Henry Adams wrote, "was a false one." Hay, a friend and contemporary of Roosevelt's father, was twenty years older than his chief and was never really comfortable serving the exuberant young President, whom he remembered as the child he had once held on his knee. Roosevelt, who was fond of Hay, admired him, and at one time even called him "the greatest Secretary of State I have seen in my time," graciously tried to sweep away the difference in their ages, but he would not rely on Hay to the extent that McKinley had. He allowed Hay to administer the State Department and direct some negotiations, but he himself originated policy, often without consulting his Secretary of State. Disliking the formal channels of diplomacy leading through the State Department, Roosevelt frequently engaged directly in negotiations and other aspects of diplomacy, thus circumventing his Secretary. These attempts to monopolize power irked Hay.

Roosevelt justified his direct control of foreign affairs by saying that "when a matter is of capital importance, it is well to have it handled by one man" and that Hay was a weakling who sometimes could not be trusted. This criticism was partly true, for the Secretary was an Anglophile and something of a Germanophobe (he referred to William II of Germany as "His Awfulness"). "He had grown to hate the Kaiser so," the President remarked of Hay, "that I could not trust him in dealing with Germany." Later, he wrote that "Hay could not be trusted where England was concerned." At another time, Roosevelt said that in the work of the State Department, "I had to do the big things myself, and the other things I have always feared would be badly done or not done at all."

During Hay's last two years in office, the President was compelled to take over direct control of foreign affairs because the Secretary was frequently sick. In fact, in the months before his death, Hay was Secretary in name only. As Roosevelt explained, "for a number of months now I have had to be my own Secretary of State, and while I am very glad to be it so far as the broad outlines of the work are concerned, I of course ought not to have to attend to the details."

After Hay's death and a private printing of his letters in which there were comments Roosevelt disliked, the Rough Rider reversed his earlier estimate, saying that Hay "was not a great Secretary of State." His Secretary's usefulness, he wrote, "was almost the usefulness of a fine figurehead." Hay, he insisted, "never initiated a policy or was of real assistance in carrying thru a policy; but he sometimes phrased what I desired said in a way that was a real service; and the respect for him was such that his presence in the Cabinet was a strength to the administration."

Even though Roosevelt's evaluation of Hay is excessively harsh, the Secretary obviously did not possess much power over the conduct of foreign relations; he was more a diplomat than a statesman. Thus, we have another example of a Secretary of State who stands out as a maker of policy under one President and is reduced almost to the status of a polished administrative assistant under another.

II.

Like Theodore Roosevelt, Woodrow Wilson was a President determined to act as virtually his own foreign minister, one who found it difficult to delegate authority. "He is," one of his Cabinet members observed, "one of those men made to tread the winepress alone. The opportunity comes now and then to give a suggestion or to utter a word of warning, but on the whole I feel that he probably is less dependent on others than any President of our time." Two of Wilson's Secretaries of State, in part at least as a result of his independence, functioned, in many instances, practically as figureheads.

Although Wilson consulted his first Secretary, William Jennings Bryan, on various subjects and even allowed him independence in shaping some policies—in the Caribbean and in a project to advance peace through a world-wide network of conciliation agreements, or "cooling-off" treaties—in most matters, he did not permit Bryan the power of initiative. Wilson himself exercised a tight control over the conduct of foreign relations, a control that Bryan at first did not question. Unlike some other Secretaries, Bryan accepted his subordinate position gracefully and seemed pleased merely with the honor of the Secretaryship. Those who knew him said he was "deferential to the office" or "highly appreciative of the position to which he had been appointed."

Bryan's honor appears an empty one, for Wilson apparently could never fully overcome his feeling that his Secretary was incapable of dealing adequately with great matters of state. Moreover, he distrusted the career officers of the State Department and often used executive agents to circumvent the department and the Secretary himself.

Wilson's personal control of foreign relations became more marked as international affairs, after 1914, came to dominate his Administration. He entered diplomatic negotiations himself, without using or even consulting his Secretary. At one time, when he sent Colonel House abroad to seek some way of mediating the war in Europe, he told House to explain to Sir Edward Grey, the British Foreign Minister, that "while you are abroad I expect to act directly through you and avoid all intermediaries."

In May, 1915, after the sinking of the British passenger liner *Lusitania*, with a high loss of American lives, Wilson, on his own initiative and without outside consultation, prepared a strong protest to the German Government. When he read it to his Cabinet, only Bryan objected. Although Wilson then softened the note a bit and Bryan signed it, that signature meant little, for the note remained Wilson's in thought and word.

The second *Lusitania* note was also Wilson's. Bryan was convinced that this note would lead to war with Germany. Rather than accept the President's policy, he resigned in an act of conscience to take the issue to the people.

In later years, Bryan resented the charge that as Secretary of State he had been a figurehead and maintained that the President had consulted him "on every proposition." Yet a Cabinet member reported being told by Mrs. Bryan at the time of her husband's resignation, "that her husband had been unhappy in his position for some time on account of the President's habit of preparing important papers himself. He had come to feel, she said, that he was not consulted as he ought to be, and that he was playing the part of a figurehead." When Bryan offered his resignation, Wilson recalled, "he had remarked with a quiver in his voice and of his lips, 'Colonel House has been Secretary of State, not I, and I have never had your full confidence.'"

The fact seems to be that Bryan was far from being the "Mr. Prime Minister" his friends had called him. Although a kindlier chief than Polk, Wilson, too, in many ways had reduced the Secretaryship almost to the status of a high-level clerkship.

Under Robert Lansing, the next Secretary of State, the office seemingly became even more of a clerkship than it had been under Bryan. Ironically, Wilson had at first opposed Lansing because he lacked imagination and initiative, but Colonel House urged his appointment. "I have a feeling," House had told the President, "that if Lansing is at all acceptable to you that he could be used to better advantage than a stronger man."

House, in fact, had suggested a reorganization of the State Department that would give it two new assistant secretaries. "These with Lansing," he explained to Wilson, "would be able to do the details intelligently, and you could direct as heretofore and without half the annoyance and anxiety that you have been under." It was most important, he advised, "to get a man with not too many ideas of his own and one that will be entirely guided by you without unnecessary argument, and this, it seems to me, you would find in Lansing."

Wilson agreed, but Lansing himself was convinced that the President appointed him because he thought they were of the same mind concerning international affairs. Others believed Wilson had told Lansing that as Secretary he would function essentially as a legal clerk. Wilson's son-in-law, Secretary of the Treasury William G. McAdoo, said that Lansing "accepted his post with a distinct understanding that all negotiations with foreign powers were to be carried on by the President." Postmaster General Albert Burleson pointed out that "Wilson is going to be his own Secretary of State. Lansing is the very man he wants—a good lawyer, without outstanding personality, who will be able to carry on the regular duties of the office and be perfectly willing for the 'Old Man' to be the real Secretary of State."

Even outsiders, *The Nation*, for example, held similar views. "Every President," it said, "has to be, in the big matters, his own Secretary of State, and Mr. Wilson will undoubtedly continue to determine for himself the main features of our foreign policy."

These estimates of Lansing's status proved fairly accurate. He came to be the silent man of the Cabinet. In meetings, he rarely spoke, did not attempt to influence policy openly in any area, except possibly foreign relations, and was so deferential to the President's views that the other department heads were convinced he had no ideas of his own. Lansing did have his own ideas but usually could not persuade Wilson to accept them.

The relations between Lansing and Wilson were always more or less formal, and the Secretary never knew what went on in the President's mind, in fact, never understood him. Wilson seldom sought his Secretary's advice on matters of policy and continued to write some of his own notes, but, as expected, he relied on Lansing's expert knowledge of international law and his other technical skills in the drafting of most notes and documents. Lansing's lack of influence on important issues was so obvious that it led the German Ambassador to declare that "since Wilson decides *everything,* any interview with Lansing is a mere matter of form."

In the diplomacy of World War I, and especially the peace-making, Wilson practically ignored his Secretary of State. In drawing up his Fourteen Points for peace, in January, 1918, for instance, the President obtained his ideas and information from the "Inquiry," a group of experts that had been organized by Colonel House to deal with the problems of the peace. Wilson did not show his Secretary the Fourteen Points address until the day before he was to deliver it and then allowed Lansing to make only a few slight changes that did not affect its substance. Later, Colonel House, not the President, informed Lansing of the general plans for the Paris Peace Conference.

Wilson would even have excluded the Secretary from the Peace Commission that went to Paris if he had not felt that he had to include him because the other foreign ministers would be active in their delegations. To have left Lansing at home, moreover, would have been an unpardonable affront.

At the conference, Lansing took virtually no part in drawing up the Treaty of Versailles or in shaping the League of Nations. Before the Peace Commission had left for Paris, he did not even know of Wilson's plan for the League. The President, he wrote, "neither asked my advice as to any provision of the [League] Covenant nor discussed the subject with me personally." Lansing was able to gain some information from Colonel House, but his first basic knowledge came from the President in a conversation on the ship that carried them to Europe.

On one occasion in Paris when the Secretary tried to take the initiative, the President rebuffed him. Without consulting Wilson beforehand, Lansing asked the legal advisers to the American Commission to prepare an outline treaty for the Commission's use. When the President learned of it, he told his Secretary, "I don't want lawyers drafting this treaty."

"I was deeply incensed at this intemperate remark," Lansing recorded, "as he knew I was a lawyer. . . . I never forgot his words and always felt that in his mind my opinions, even when he sought them, were tainted with legalism."

In February, 1919, when Wilson had to return to Washington before the close of Congress, Lansing as Secretary of State stood to inherit the official leadership of the American delegation, but the President acted so as to place actual authority in the hands of Colonel House and to make Lansing merely titular head *ad interim.* Wilson not only distrusted his Secretary, he also wished to retain direct control of negotiations. Consequently, he wanted decisions postponed until he returned to Paris. "It showed very clearly," Lansing wrote, "that the President intended to do everything himself and to allow no one to act for him unless it was upon some highly technical matter."

Seven months later, after Wilson's collapse at Pueblo, Colorado, Lansing was left in sole charge of the State Department, but again he was allowed no power of decision in matters of policy. The sick President either refused to answer his Secretary's recommendations or vetoed them. "He is certainly well enough to interfere with or nullify everything I attempt to do," Lansing complained.

The Secretary said that if it were not for the President's illness, he would have resigned. "I want to be free and my own master," he wrote. "I am sick of being treated as a school boy or a rubber stamp." When he finally did resign, he explained that he had been conscious of the fact that Wilson did not welcome his "advice in matters pertaining to the negotiations in Paris, to our foreign service, or to international affairs in general."

So bitter did Lansing become over his ignominious status that he denounced the President as "a tyrant, who even goes so far as to demand that all men shall *think* as he does or else be branded as traitors or ingrates." We can see, therefore, that Wilson had made a mistake in selecting Lansing for the part of a figurehead. Few Secretaries of State, in fact, have suffered such frustration and helplessness as did Lansing. He left office detesting the man who had raised him to the highest appointive post in the land.

III.

Even more than in the case of Lansing, the conditions under which Cordell Hull—the next Secretary of State who at times had merely nominal authority over the conduct of foreign relations—accepted office are clouded with contradictions. According to one story, he was advised to accept only on the condition that Franklin D. Roosevelt would allow him to make his own appointments in the State Department. "The Secretary," he was told, "should at least be given every chance to have the personal loyalty of his assistants." Hull appeared to take this advice but then accepted the post without insisting upon control over appointments. This, the story goes, was a fatal mistake.

Hull himself asserted, however, that he did lay down conditions before taking Roosevelt's offer. He said that he sought and was able to obtain a complete understanding that he would be more than a mere administrative clerk. "If I accept the Secretaryship of State," he told Roosevelt, "I do not have in mind the mere carrying on of correspondence with foreign governments." He insisted upon being consulted and having a share "in the formulation and conduct of foreign policy." Roosevelt, according to Hull, agreed to the conditions and assured him that "we shall function in the manner you've stated."

Whether or not Hull accepted the Secretaryship under firm conditions that he himself had set, his record reveals that he came to have only a small part in the shaping of major foreign policies. He claimed that the President allowed him considerable independence and "that in the majority of cases I had to make my own decisions," but critics maintain, with some exaggeration, that he was in fact little more than an "imposing white-haired figurehead." It is true that in some matters, such as in a program for reciprocal trade agreements, in Latin American affairs, and in negotiations with Japan prior to the attack on Pearl Harbor, the Secretary had substantial influence; in most instances, however, his power of decision appears to have extended mainly over administrative procedure and the mass of detail that daily flowed into the State Department. Roosevelt, the evidence shows, often chose to act as his own foreign minister.

From the beginning, the President himself made the basic appointments in the State Department and Foreign Service. He corresponded privately with diplomats in the field, carried on direct negotiations with foreign statesmen, and made most of the important policy decisions on his own. In effect, he frequently acted without seeking the advice of his Secretary of State.

At the World Economic Conference, in London, in the summer of 1933, the Secretary of State was the *ex officio* chairman of the American delegation, but Roosevelt had chosen the delegates without consulting him. Hull had no real power over them and could not instruct them or prevent them from making embarrassing statements to the press. His role was so humiliating that even though he had been in office only a few months, he considered resigning.

In that same year, against Hull's wishes, Roosevelt sent an invitation directly to the President of the Soviet Union calling for negotiations over the terms of American recognition of the Communist regime. When Hull's negotiations deadlocked, the President stepped in, and in what he called man-to-man talks with the Russians, concluded a recognition agreement.

Direct diplomacy became something of a habit with Roosevelt. In September, 1938, when Adolf Hitler threatened Czechoslovakia, William C. Bullitt, Ambassador to France and one of the several friends of Roosevelt who did not hesitate to go over Hull's head, urged the President to attempt to preserve peace by appealing directly to the heads of the governments involved in the crisis. Sumner Welles also urged the appeal. Hull opposed it, saying later that "Welles kept pushing the President on while I kept advising him to go slow." Siding with Bullitt and Welles, the President made the appeal.

Seven months later, after Benito Mussolini's Italian Blackshirts had invaded Albania, Bullitt telephoned Roosevelt from Paris urging him to ask Hitler and Mussolini to guarantee specific countries against attack. As before, Hull opposed the idea. "It was another of the direct appeals to the heads of Government, in which practice," he wrote, "I had little confidence." Again the President ignored the advice of his Secretary and made the appeal.

The fact that the advice of subordinates like Bullitt carried greater weight with the President than did the Secretary's weakened Hull's influence in the Cabinet and in his own department. The fact that his subordinates could correspond directly with the President had the same effect. Admiral William D. Leahy, for example, regularly wrote directly to Roosevelt, and thus circumvented the Secretary of State, when he was Ambassador to the Vichy Government of France.

Roosevelt's direct diplomacy also eroded his Secretary's influence with foreign statesmen. Shrewd ones, like Russia's Constantine Oumansky, were convinced that Hull meant well but had no control over policy. Oumansky, therefore, attempted to channel important matters directly to the President.

No other foreign statesman, however, went over Hull's head as often as did Winston Churchill, who all during the years of World War II carried on high-level diplomacy directly with Roosevelt—much of it unknown to the Secretary of State. He and Roosevelt, for instance, handled the details in the exchange of British bases for American destroyers in 1940. Almost up to the time the executive agreement was completed, Hull, in fact, opposed it, arguing "that the President had no authority to give away Government property."

Roosevelt and Churchill also planned the Atlantic Conference of 1941 without Hull's knowledge. When the Secretary returned to Washington from a vacation, he found that "the President was already en route to his rendezvous."

Later that year, when the Prime Minister visited Roosevelt in Washington, he and Hull clashed over British and American policy toward the Free French Government of General Charles de Gaulle. The Secretary felt that the British were undermining the policy he had established toward the Free French, but Hull's anger did not disturb Churchill. The Secretary, Churchill wrote, "did not seem to me to have full access to the President."

To Hull's consternation, the President also deliberately excluded him from the other wartime "summit" conferences—Casablanca, Cairo, and Teheran. Hull protested his exclusion: "I'm not looking for increased responsibility, but I do believe the Secretary of State should attend these meetings." To strengthen his case he pointed out that the British Foreign Secretary participated in various war councils.

The President replied that the British governmental system differed from the American in that the British Cabinet constituted the government. Under the parliamentary system, the Foreign Secretary had stronger claims than had the Secretary of State to participation in the war councils, particularly when vital diplomatic problems were considered. Roosevelt pointed out, in effect, that under the Presidential system, he could do virtually as he pleased in the conduct of foreign relations.

Roosevelt did not, however, completely disregard Hull's feelings. He stressed that the wartime conferences were essentially military, not diplomatic, and hence did not require the Secretary's presence. Yet, he did not inform Hull even of the diplomatic developments, leaving him in ignorance of what went on at the meetings. "I learned from other sources than the President," the Secretary wrote, "what had occurred at the Casablanca, Cairo, and Tehran conferences." Discussing with Henry Morgenthau what would follow the Teheran Conference, in 1944, Hull gasped, according to Morgenthau, and said, "Henry, this is the first time I have ever heard of this. . . . I have never even been permitted to see the minutes of the Tehran conference!"

So determined was Roosevelt to deprive Hull of any tangible reason for attending the summit meetings that he sometimes went to extremes. One of the reasons he kept his advisory party small at those conferences was to freeze out his Secretary of State. When Churchill, for example, agreed to the Casablanca Conference, he told Roosevelt that he wanted to take Anthony Eden with him because of his position as a member of the British War

Cabinet as well as the fact that he was Foreign Secretary. Realizing that if Eden were included, Hull would have a good excuse to attend also, the President objected and made it a firm condition that Eden be excluded.

Hull's exclusion from the conferences fell in with Roosevelt's general design of subordinating the State Department to other agencies involved in wartime diplomacy. Before the United States had entered the war, Hull had been a member of the War Council—a small inner group composed of the President; the Secretaries of State, War, and Navy; the Chief of Staff; and the Chief of Naval Operations—and had regularly attended its meetings. After the attack on Pearl Harbor, the President shut him out of the meetings concerned with military matters and never informed him, for example, of the atomic-bomb project.

Realizing that there could be no war council that did not in some way deal with diplomatic matters, Hull occasionally questioned his exclusion, but he could bring about no change in his status.

Another technique that Roosevelt used in circumscribing the authority of his Secretary of State was to create new agencies and entrust them with responsibilities in foreign affairs. He neither consulted Hull in forming them nor allowed him control over them. Often administrators of the agencies clashed with the Secretary in various jurisdictional disputes.

One of those agencies, the Office of Lend-Lease Administration, became a vital bond in America's relations with the other Allied governments and with some of the neutral nations, as well. Increasingly, therefore, foreign missions in the United States directed or tried to direct much of their important business to the head of that agency rather than to the Secretary of State. Furthermore, Lend-Lease ignored the Foreign Service by sending its own representatives abroad.

W. Averell Harriman, for instance, went to London as "Expediter" of Lend-Lease with the rank of Minister. He had direct access to Churchill and Roosevelt and did not even use State Department channels to report to his chief, Harry Hopkins.

Occasionally, Hopkins sent Hull polite notes with enclosed cables marked "For your information." Being brought up to date on foreign relations in this manner did not soothe Hull's injured pride.

Thus, many of the important matters of policy did not go to the Secretary for decision, and much of the President's diplomacy never went through the State Department. Many of the department's upper-level career officers, Roosevelt believed, had been abroad too long, had lost the feel of their own country, and were not truly representative of the American people or the objectives of his Administration.

Hull, on the other hand, accepted the State Department as he found it and became its ardent defender. He also often opposed the President's views or was slow in giving them support. It was for these and other reasons that Roosevelt frequently excluded his Secretary from the formulation of important policies. Furthermore, he lost patience with Hull's conservatism, especially during the war, when he felt that quick daring action was needed in the management of foreign relations. Paradoxically, therefore, as foreign relations became increasingly vital, the Secretary of State became less important in their conduct.

Hull's lack of pervasive influence can also be seen in the fact that his relations with Roosevelt were largely official and devoted mostly to routine State Department affairs. The President usually did not discuss domestic affairs with him. Since he was not in the inner circle of advisers, Hull's social contacts with the President were also limited. "I was frankly glad," the Secretary wrote, perhaps with a sour-grapes attitude, "not to be invited into the White House groups where so often the 'liberal' game was played on an extreme basis."

The Secretary, moreover, was unable to use the Cabinet to influence policy, for Roosevelt seldom discussed international affairs in the Cabinet meetings. "Roosevelt Cabinets are really a solo performance by the President," one department head explained, "interspersed with some questions and very few debates."

Hull himself wrote that "no decisions on foreign policy were taken by Cabinet vote during my tenure."

Although Hull resented his status, he did not hold the bitterness toward Roosevelt that Lansing felt toward Wilson. He apparently realized that he held an office of great prestige but without the full power that should have gone with it. Having held office most of his life, he also realized that some of the indignities he suffered were inevitable in public life and hence apparently bore them as occupational hazards.

Hull told a friend at the end of his Secretaryship:

> When I accepted this office, I knew that I would be misrepresented, lied about, let down, and that there would be humiliations that no man in private life could accept and keep his self-respect. But I made up my mind in advance that I would accept all these things and just do my job. I have suffered all these things but have just kept right on.

He kept on, in fact, for almost twelve years, longer than any other Secretary of State.

Despite Hull's sometimes nominal control over foreign relations, he was not publicly reduced to a figurehead and was never denied control over his own department—because he had considerable political influence. He was, in fact, the most popular department head in the Roosevelt Administration (especially with conservatives), as a Gallup poll published in 1938 indicated. Roosevelt, moreover, always publicly treated him with respect, acclaiming him the "father" of the United Nations and recommending him for the Nobel Peace Prize. Hull's tenure shows that the Secretaryship, under certain conditions, can bring distinction even to one who seems almost a figurehead, and that even so dynamic a President as Franklin D. Roosevelt was not truly "his own Secretary of State."

Roosevelt's next Secretary, Edward R. Stettinius, Jr., was expected to carry out the President's own policies without objection and to advance no ideas of his own. In urging his appointment, Harry Hopkins had argued, in effect, that since the President would continue his high-level personal diplomacy and would manage foreign relations on his own, he needed only a figurehead in the Secretaryship and that Stettinius would fit this role graciously.

Although Stettinius did not attempt to initiate policy, by the time he took office, the gulf between the President and the State Department had become so great that he decided to appoint a career officer for liaison between the department and the White House. "This was an effort by Stettinius," one of Roosevelt's advisers wrote, "to get in closer contact with the President, who had been handling much foreign affairs business without consulting the Department of State."

Although it seemed strange for the Secretary to need an intermediary between himself and the President, Stettinius did manage to develop a closer relationship with Roosevelt than had Hull. He was told about the secret atomic-bomb project and was taken to the Yalta Conference, but had no truly important function there. In the eleven months that Stettinius held the Secretaryship, he served, as Hopkins had predicted, mainly as an agent who faithfully carried out the President's own policies.

Unlike Stettinius, Dean Rusk is not a figurehead and is respected by the President for his grasp of foreign affairs. Yet within a few months after Rusk had taken office, critics began pointing out that he apparently was not the central figure in the shaping of foreign policy. For instance, he was reported to have opposed American support for an ill-fated invasion of Cuba, in April, 1961, but the President apparently preferred the views of others. To the public, Rusk in his first year in office seemed overshadowed by a coterie of White House advisers on foreign policy and by politically powerful princelings in his own department. Some argued that these advisers stood between President Kennedy and Rusk and hence encroached upon the power that should belong to the Secretary. The dynamic Kennedy himself, moreover, on most issues seems to take direct command of foreign relations and hence keeps his Secretary of State in the shadows.

Regardless of the cause, lack of power in the Secretaryship is not unusual. The very nature of the office allows the President to use his Secretary of State almost as a figurehead if he so desires and if the Secretary accepts such a status. If the President contents himself with such a Secretary, he adds immeasurably to the burdens of his office and deprives himself of normal assistance in the conduct of foreign relations, the area of his gravest responsibility. If he does not accept the Secretary of State as his principal adviser, primary executive agent, and trusted confidant in foreign affairs, one of the basic relationships in the American system of government will not function as effectively as it should. In other words, a President who insists on acting as his own Secretary of State is like a pilot who fails to obtain maximum power from his airplane because he refuses to use all of its engines.

6

The Partnership

The foreign affairs are in their inception and management exclusively executive, and nothing decisive can
be done in that important field except with the President's personal knowledge and official approval. So
entirely confidential has the relation of the Secretary to
the President been held that questions relating to foreign affairs are brought to the attention of other members of the Cabinet by the Secretary of State *only* as
directed by the President.
                                        —JAMES G. BLAINE, 1889

SOME Secretaries of State have managed to remain on good
terms with the President without becoming figureheads and,
in effect, to control the conduct of foreign relations without attempting to act as prime ministers. This, recent analysts maintain,
is essentially what the intensely personal relationship between
the President and the Secretary should be—one of partnership.
It cannot, of course, be a partnership of equals, but rather of a
junior and a senior colleague.

Nevertheless, in the case of John Marshall, the first strong
Secretary of this type, critics have charged that he had gained an
unhealthy ascendancy over the President who came to rely heavily on him for aid in domestic as well as foreign affairs and who,
they said, would accept his Secretary's ideas without realizing
that he did. John Adams, it seemed, had such confidence in
Marshall that almost from the time the Virginian took over the
Secretaryship, he received a mandate to run other parts of the

government as well as the State Department, and hence became a Secretary who carried a larger share of responsibility than had his predecessors.

Marshall came to assume this broad responsibility not only because Adams trusted him, but also because soon after he became Secretary, the President left the seat of government for his home in Quincy, Massachusetts, and remained there during most of the eight months Marshall held office. The Secretary, therefore, seemingly ran the government like perhaps a viceroy, taking his orders from a distance. He did not, however, attempt to use this circumstance indiscriminately to make his own ideas policy or to impose his will upon the President, but instead trimmed his ideas to fit his chief's policies. Marshall, in fact, had faith in those policies and carefully carried them out as Adams desired—a key factor in his success, one that gave him power, brought strength to the Administration, and won favor with the President.

The next Secretary of State, James Madison, was much closer to Thomas Jefferson than Marshall had been to Adams. Madison was one of Jefferson's old friends, whom the President could trust to carry out his policies as he desired. Few Secretaries and Presidents have been able to work together with so intimate an understanding of each other's views as did Madison and Jefferson. So close did the collaboration appear that certain contemporaries believed that Jefferson had formed the habit of trusting "almost implicitly in Madison," and that the Secretary had "acquired a compleat ascendancy over him." To some, it seemed that the President scarcely consulted the other department heads.

It is improbable that Madison enjoyed the ascendancy alleged to him, for although the President listened to his advice and frequently changed his views as a result, Jefferson made his own decisions, and the policies Madison directed were clearly the President's. Madison proved himself a valuable administrator and adviser, one who offered counsel when needed or requested, in domestic as well as foreign affairs, but who functioned as a Secretary who realized and accepted his subordination to the President's will.

In this capacity, Madison had responsibility for the conduct of the nation's foreign relations for eight years—the first Secretary of State to complete two full Presidential terms. When his Presidency closed, Jefferson declared that "Mr. Madison is justly entitled to his full share of all the measures of my administration. Our principles were the same, and we never differed sensibly in the application of them."

Eight years later, John Quincy Adams took over the Secretaryship, also clearly realizing that he must function as a subordinate and that his duty required him to support, and not in any way counteract, the President's policies. This, he believed, would not be difficult, for he was convinced that his views coincided with the President's. He wrote of the relationship he envisaged:

> The President, I am sure, will neither require nor expect from me any sacrifice of principles inconsistent with my own sense of right, and I hope I shall never be unmindful of the respect for his character, the deference to his sentiments, and the attachment to his person, due from me to him, not only by the relative situation which he has placed me to himself, but by the gratitude with which his kindness ought to be requited.

Despite this deference to the President, Adams is one of the few Secretaries of State who has been given most of the credit for what was accomplished in foreign affairs during his term. This recognition of his talent seems especially remarkable when one considers the fact that James Monroe had had extensive diplomatic experience, nearly six years in the Secretaryship himself, and was not a President who readily surrendered control of foreign policy to anyone.

Although Monroe listened to his Secretary's views and frequently was swayed by them, he made it clear that he alone was responsible for the foreign policy of his Administration, a responsibility he willingly assumed. He read most of the important dispatches that came into the State Department and went over Adams' drafts, modifying, enlarging, or cutting them down. In some instances he drafted notes himself or told his Secretary exactly what he wanted written. In effect, he kept his finger on every diplomatic decision of consequence. "This sifting and revising of every important paper that I write," Adams once complained, "is not flattering nor very agreeable."

Monroe also maintained a tight control over appointments, causing Adams to lament his lack of influence. "The President," he said in reference to the pattern of appointments, "kept it very much in his own hands. There had not been a single appointment of any consequence, even in my own Department, made at my recommendation, nor one that I approved."

Yet, Monroe never ignored his Secretary's opinions and, within the limits mentioned, allowed him broad power in the conduct of foreign relations. Adams knew what was going on in the Administration and frequently his ideas became policy. Even though he maintained that, with few exceptions, he deferred to the President, he expressed his views forcibly, fought for his own policies, and held firmly to them against competing advice. Furthermore, particularly when he considered an issue important, he did not hesitate to offer unsolicited and independent advice. These are the qualities of a dynamic Secretary of State, but not necessarily of one who functioned like a prime minister. Only when a President delegates big areas of his power to a Secretary of State, which Monroe would not do, can the Secretary be considered something of a prime minister.

All in all, Adams and Monroe made an effective team. "They were made for each other," Jefferson is said to have observed. "Adams has a pointed pen; Monroe has judgment enough for both and firmness enough to have *his* judgment control." The secret of this successful relationship seems to be that from the beginning, both Monroe and Adams understood who was President in fact as well as in title—a principle basic to a really effective partnership.

The next Secretary of State who came to hold an influential place in government without aspiring to the power of a premier was William M. Evarts. He never approached Adams in accomplishment and, in fact, is one of the lesser-known Secretaries, one who dealt with no great international problems. Political opponents, nonetheless, deplored his alleged influence. One of them claimed that "his dreamy doctrines have captivated the President and led him into many of his unfortunate ways that have done much to alienate his friends." Others pictured him as the Mephistopheles of the Cabinet, who held Rutherford B. Hayes—whom they called "His Fraudulency the President"—his captive.

Although in domestic as well as foreign affairs Evarts' views carried weight with the President, they were not decisive. Hayes himself usually controlled the conduct of foreign relations and made the decisions in policy. Evarts, moreover, wisely did not attempt to force his ideas upon the President. In general, he and Hayes respected each other and enjoyed each other's company. When Evarts took office, he and the President hardly knew each other, but they soon got along so well that by the time he gave up the Secretaryship, he and Hayes had become close friends.

Like Hayes, Grover Cleveland got along well with his Secretaries of State. In his two terms in the White House, he had three Secretaries and not one functioned either as a figurehead or as a prime minister. In working with all three, Cleveland accepted and often followed their advice, but he himself took a hand in all important questions of foreign policy and, depending on the Secretary, made most of the decisions. He also decided on most of the diplomatic appointments himself and, if he believed such action necessary, did so without consulting his Secretary.

Thomas F. Bayard, Cleveland's first Secretary, frequently influenced foreign policy, but usually acted as the instrument of the President's wishes instead of an initiator of policy. He was one of Cleveland's favorite companions, one who constantly visited the White House and was consulted on many matters besides foreign affairs. Cleveland greatly admired Bayard and once said, "I think he is one of the most complete men, mentally, morally, and politically, I ever met."

The next Secretary, Walter Q. Gresham, acquired more power over foreign relations than had Bayard. Cleveland developed a strong affection for him and consulted him on almost all matters pertaining to international affairs and on many domestic problems. Gresham's influence was such that Cleveland more often than not followed his suggestions, and the Secretary thus in effect initiated policy.

Cleveland relied more for advice and guidance on his third Secretary, Richard Olney, than he had on either Bayard or Gresham and allowed Olney considerable freedom in the conduct of foreign relations. For instance, when Olney drew up his first important state paper as Secretary of State—a bold note dealing with a sensitive boundary dispute between Venezuela and British Guiana—Cleveland commended him for preparing "the best thing of the kind I have ever read."

The President, in fact, left the details of the diplomacy of the Venezuelan controversy "wholly in Mr. Olney's hands." The Secretary antagonized Great Britain and drafted a warlike message that the President revised and sent to Congress in December, 1895. Despite the criticism the message evoked, Cleveland defended it and praised his Secretary.

Cleveland later told a friend:

> I do not think that, in all my experience, I have ever had to deal with any official document, prepared by another, which so entirely satisfied my critical requirements. . . . It was vigorous, but it caught the national spirit perfectly. I have never been able to express my pleasure and satisfaction over this assertion of our position, and the country has never shown that it fairly understood or recognized the debt it owes to Richard Olney.

Even though Olney exerted substantial influence on the President in both external and internal affairs, he did not seek the power of a prime minister. He regarded himself as the President's personal adviser, a zealous and important member of Cleveland's official family. Not being a professional politician looking forward to greater rewards, Olney took the Secretaryship as an end in itself. He often ignored political considerations in arriving at decisions and made no effort to placate party factions, but instead tried to make the most of the Secretaryship within the scope of its limited powers. Although he served only twenty-one months, Olney showed that even under a strong President, a forceful Secretary of State need not function as a prime minister in order to have a decisive voice in the shaping of foreign policy.

Unlike Olney, John Hay cannot be considered a forceful Secretary of State, but under McKinley he, too, had a hand in shaping foreign policy without assuming himself a premier. Ironically, he accepted the Secretaryship unwillingly, as a duty he would gladly have avoided if he could have done so gracefully, or at least he went out of his way to give that impression. "I am a soldier," he said, "and go where I am sent."

Yet, Hay looked upon McKinley with affection and respect and worked amiably with him. In fact, the two men were quite close. Often they would make decisions in conference, and would work together on diplomatic notes, correcting and polishing each other's drafts. Although the President kept a firm control over the general direction of foreign policy and did not hesitate to make his own decisions, he usually followed his Secretary's advice and allowed him broad discretion in the conduct of foreign relations. "He has been most generous and liberal ever since I have been here," Hay said of his chief; "he has allowed me an absolutely free hand in the important work of the Department, supporting and sustaining me in the face of all sorts of opposition in Congress and elsewhere."

The President, however, did not share his control over appointments. "As to appointments under the State Department," Hay wrote, perhaps in exaggeration, "it is clear that I am to have nothing to say. I could not appoint even my Private Secretary." At another time he remarked, "I have not controlled a single appointment in the State Department since I entered it."

Hay did, however, express his own views on some appointments and the President listened, for he respected Hay. So highly did McKinley esteem his Secretary that in March, 1900, when Hay offered his resignation over a quarrel with Congress, the President refused it and returned it the day it was submitted. "Nothing could be more unfortunate than to have you retire from the

Cabinet," McKinley wrote privately. "The personal loss would be great but the public loss even greater. Your administration of the State Department has had my warm approval." It was under this kind of a relationship with the President, essentially that of a partnership, that Hay acquired his reputation as one of the nation's distinguished Secretaries of State.

Elihu Root, who had been an outstanding Secretary of War, never achieved Hay's distinction in the Secretaryship of State, but he too was a Secretary who was able to win more than the usual share of the President's confidence. That confidence was based on a close friendship and mutual respect between himself and Theodore Roosevelt. Root did not insist upon launching policies of his own, did not appear to push pet policies that were clearly distinguishable from the President's, and accepted Roosevelt's close control of foreign relations without resenting it. In directing those foreign relations, Root worked mainly as the agent who carried out the President's own policies.

Roosevelt, however, did not use Root merely as an administrative assistant. He relied upon his Secretary for careful advice. In later years, moreover, Root himself declared that Roosevelt "was the most advisable" man he ever knew. In some areas, in Latin American affairs, for example, Root had virtually unhampered responsibility for matters of policy. "My part in it," Roosevelt said, "has been little beyond cordially backing him up." Furthermore, Root did not hesitate to speak, and when he did, he gained the President's ear. Roosevelt himself pointed this out. Once when an editor asked him which of his Cabinet officers had been most valuable, "Elihu Root," Roosevelt replied. "He is the only one who will fight with me."

When Root left the Secretaryship, Roosevelt told him "that in my judgment you will be regarded as the greatest and ablest man who ever filled the position of Secretary of State." Although an exaggeration, that statement apparently expressed Roosevelt's true sentiments at the time.

The source of Root's success in winning Roosevelt's confidence seems to be that he did not allow the President to see in him a political or intellectual rival. Root accepted the Secretaryship for what it was under Roosevelt, a junior partnership, did not attempt to make it a premiership, and did not overreach himself in any grab for power.

I.

Calvin Coolidge, who seldom took the initiative in matters of foreign policy, left Secretary of State Frank B. Kellogg with the major responsibility for handling almost all problems in foreign affairs. Like Root, however, Kellogg did not attempt to seize more power. He usually originated policy and controlled its conduct, and Coolidge generally merely approved. Although nervous and upset by some of the demands of his office, Kellogg apparently was content with his status, authority, and relationship to the President. In later years, he said that the Secretaryship had given him the best and most interesting period of his life.

In contrast to Coolidge, Harry Truman was extremely sensitive to any encroachment on what he considered the responsibilities of the President, particularly in foreign affairs. Yet he allowed his Secretaries of State freedom in shaping foreign policy. He believed that the Secretary should run his own department, "but all final policy decisions," he insisted, "would be mine." He also held that "the Secretary of State should never at any time come to think that he is the man in the White House, and the President should not try to be the Secretary of State." This principle, he believed, worked exceptionally well in his relations with two of his Secretaries, George C. Marshall and Dean G. Acheson.

As far as Truman was concerned, Marshall was the ideal Secretary. It is doubtful that any President has admired his Secretary of State as deeply as did Truman. More than once, he publicly referred to Marshall as the greatest living American and wrote that the "General is one of the most astute and profound men I have ever known." Regardless of contrary pressures, Truman invariably followed Marshall's advice, often without question.

Marshall, in turn, respected Truman and, like Truman, revered the Presidency. In 1948, when Truman began his lonely whistle-stop election campaign against great odds, Marshall was one of the loyal department heads who saw him off and wished him well. During that campaign, as at other times, the Secretary resisted the suggestions of some of his career subordinates that foreign policy was independent of the President. Unlike some of the other Cabinet officers, he remained loyal to Truman the man as well as Truman the President.

Truman never forgot this loyalty. He depended on Marshall because he could rely on him, knowing that the Secretary would carry out policy as he desired. He knew, too, that Marshall, unlike some of his other appointees, did not covet the Presidency. Nor did the Secretary, as Truman believed Byrnes had, consider himself a premier.

Even though in a few instances Marshall and Truman differed over details of foreign policy, their relations were never marred by fundamental disagreement or personal conflict. More than most Secretaries of State, Marshall directly influenced the formulating of foreign policy, and far more than most Presidents, Truman went out of his way to follow his Secretary's advice. Marshall had a voice in every major decision and through his staff usually initiated policy. The President, for instance, insisted that the European Recovery Program be called the Marshall Plan because, he said, "I wanted General Marshall to get full credit for his brilliant contributions to the measure which he helped formulate."

Marshall's authority stemmed mainly from the President's unbounded faith in him, not from any desire of his own to augment his power or that of his office. As a result, even Secretaries who have aspired to the power of a prime minister could seldom match Marshall's influence over the making of foreign policy. Under him, the Secretaryship was part of a true partnership.

Like Marshall, Acheson was another of those Secretaries of State who had a decisive influence in the making of foreign policy without trying to be a premier. Since Truman himself lacked broad experience or training in foreign affairs, he came to rely heavily on Acheson, even more so than on Marshall, to keep him informed and to guide him. Acheson saw the President at least four times a week on business, and sometimes every day. At least twice a week, and more often in times of crisis, he brought or had sent to the White House carefully prepared reviews of international developments. His reports were full and clear, designed only for the President and written specifically to hold his attention. Acheson went out of his way to demonstrate that he knew and respected the fact that the President and not the Secretary of State was responsible for the conduct of foreign relations.

This constant concern for the President's sanction is one of the distinctive features of Acheson's Secretaryship. Far more than most Secretaries, as a consequence, he became the President's advocate and came to incur all the responsibilities and liabilities that such a specialized relationship entailed. Although many criticized Acheson, few, as a result, doubted his authority to speak for the Administration. He, and no one else, was the President's spokesman for foreign affairs.

On almost all issues, moreover, even where he might have disagreed, Acheson supported the President. Truman wrote, with only slight exaggeration:

> There was never a day during the four years of Dean Acheson's secretaryship that anyone could have said that he and I differed on policy. He was meticulous in keeping me posted on every development within the wide area of his responsibility. He had a deep understanding of the President's position in our constitutional scheme and realized to the fullest that, while I leaned on him for constant advice, the policy had to be mine—it was.

Thus, although the President delegated wide authority to Acheson in the conduct of foreign relations, the Secretary appears to have no truly personal record. Few knew which decisions were his, which belonged to the President, or which came from State Department subordinates. It is clear, however, that the President and his Secretary worked closely, as a partnership should. During the Korean War, the most important single crisis of Acheson's

Secretaryship, the President usually followed his advice in matters of policy despite intense pressures to do otherwise. Even when the Secretary spoke within the National Security Council, he often led the discussions and offered the advice that the President acted upon.

Truman accepted Acheson's counsel because he had faith in his judgment and ability and, like many Presidents who were pleased with their Secretaries of State, praised him without restraint. "History, I am sure," Truman wrote, "will list Dean Acheson among the truly great Secretaries of State our nation has had." And, he added, "his keen mind, cool temper, and broad vision served him well for handling the day-to-day business of the great issues of policy as well as the Department of State." Acheson, like Marshall, furthermore, had given Truman loyalty as well as service.

That loyalty worked two ways, for in his final news conference before leaving the Secretaryship, Acheson expressed deep gratitude for the complete loyalty Truman had given him. Truman had also given him power, for through Acheson's persuasive influence on the President, the Secretaryship in effect had been the source of most foreign policy.

Acheson's deference to Truman illustrates a principle that usually governs the relationship between a competent Secretary of State and a sensitive President. If the Secretary wishes to remain on good terms with such a President, he should not attempt to overshadow him. He should not try to dramatize his own actions and accomplishments and thereby steal headlines from the President; he should not act as though he were the senior partner. Violation of this code can be, and has been, a source of friction between the two men.

John C. Calhoun, for instance, tried to buck the tradition that the Secretary exists only in the shadow of the President, and in so doing caused trouble. He took office not with the idea of serving the President but mainly with the intention of advancing his own philosophy of government. After leaving the Secretaryship, moreover, he claimed credit for the outstanding accomplishment of the Tyler Administration—the annexation of Texas—a claim that the President vehemently disputed.

That determination not to be overshadowed by a prominent Secretary of State lay, in part at least, behind Polk's harsh treatment of Buchanan and Benjamin Harrison's tight control over Blaine. When Blaine was sick, as he was frequently, Harrison himself took over his duties. The President expected gratitude, but Blaine, bitter because Harrison carried out policies he disliked, offered none.

In May, 1892, Harrison aired his grievances, complaining that for over a year he had himself carried the burden of the State Department, even to preparing documents in his own handwriting. Yet, he said, Blaine had boasted of what had been done in the department and had taken all the credit. The President told a Senator that he was "perfectly willing, to use a familiar figure, to carry a soldier's knapsack, when the soldier is sore of foot and tired, and all that he wanted in return was acknowledgment of the act and a show of appreciation." Someday, he vowed, he would disclose the "true conditions" of his relations with Blaine.

A similar friction ultimately came to mar relations between Herbert Hoover and Henry L. Stimson, two men who started out their partnership with the highest respect for each other. Although Stimson did not attempt to acquire the power of a prime minister or to overshadow his chief, he did at times compete with Hoover for recognition as the maker of certain policies.

Hoover looked upon the nonrecognition doctrine of January, 1932—a doctrine that said the United States would not recognize territorial gains that violated the peace treaties—as his personal accomplishment and as the most important principle in foreign affairs advanced during his Presidency. The note announcing that principle, he told his Secretary, "would rank with the greatest papers of this country." He resented efforts, he said later, "to stamp this as the 'Stimson Doctrine' with the implication that I had no part in it."

The President was so proud of the principle that he wished to exploit it in his campaign for re-election in 1932, pointing to it as his own unique achievement. He asked Stimson, therefore, to make a speech proclaiming the nonrecognition principle as the Hoover Doctrine. Stimson would not do so, arguing that it was improper for members of the State Department to make political speeches. Moreover, he consistently refused to champion the "Hoover Doctrine," believing that the international acceptance of the nonrecognition principle, usually called the "Stimson Doctrine," was perhaps the greatest constructive achievement of his public life, an achievement he did not wish to share even with the President. "It would hurt his feelings terribly to have this called the Hoover doctrine," the Under Secretary of State noted, "because he thinks of it as one very important star which history will put to his credit."

Hoover could never overcome the feeling that his Secretary of State was trying to take credit that rightfully belonged to him. At the close of his Administration, he even obtained statements from his other department heads attesting that he, not Stimson, had been the true author of the nonrecognition doctrine.

Truman, too, felt that one of his Secretaries of State was vying with him for publicity. This feeling toward James F. Byrnes, in fact, was one cause of the break between the two men. Of the other reasons for the rupture, Truman observed:

> More and more during the fall of 1945 I came to feel that in his role as Secretary of State Byrnes was beginning to think of himself as an Assistant President in full charge of foreign policy. Apparently he failed to realize that, under the Constitution, the President is required to assume all responsibility for the conduct of foreign affairs. The President cannot abdicate that responsibility, and he cannot turn it over to anyone else.

In particular, Truman was irked by Byrnes's failure to keep him fully and privately informed of developments at a conference of foreign ministers held in Moscow in December, 1945, saying that he could learn little from his Secretary's reports that did not appear in the newspapers. After the conference, Byrnes had cabled a request to the White House to arrange time over all the radio networks so that he could explain the results of his diplomacy directly to the American people. Then he had released information on the conference to the press before reporting to the President.

According to Truman's version, one with which Byrnes disagrees, when the Secretary finally reported to him, he read the "riot act" to Byrnes.

> I told him that I did not like the way in which I had been left in the dark about the Moscow conference. I told him that, as President, I intended to know what progress we were making and what we were doing in foreign negotiations. I said it was shocking that a communiqué should be issued in Washington announcing a foreign-policy development of major importance that I had never heard of. I said I would not tolerate a repetition of such conduct.

In contrast, Eisenhower did not resent John Foster Dulles' efforts to capture attention. Indeed, he seemed to encourage them. In May, 1955, for example, Dulles reported the results of a foreign ministers' conference in Paris to the people by radio and television directly from the President's office. The President appeared with him but took only a minor part in the program. Moreover, Eisenhower tried every trick of radio and television to assure his Secretary a large audience and a chance to advertise his accomplishments in top-level diplomacy. The other members of the Cabinet, as if to emphasize the importance, pre-eminence, and unique relationship of the Secretary of State to the President, formed a mute background for Dulles' talk.

In this instance, as in others, there was never any danger that the Secretary would overshadow the President, for Eisenhower commanded such prestige that Dulles himself could gain full attention for his own accomplishments only with the President's active assistance. No Secretary of State, in fact, has profited from a President's popularity to the extent that Dulles did.

II.

The wise Secretary of State, regardless of his own fame or political influence, and even though his chief may not be the popular hero that Eisenhower was, will devote as much care to cultivating good relations with the President as he will to the policy and administrative functions of his office. He will, if he can, avoid quarrels, for it is virtually an unwritten rule that if a fight betwen a President and his Secretary becomes public knowledge, the Secretary's political career is destroyed. Seldom can the Secretary expect to wield great political influence or hold high office again.

Edmund Randolph's quarrel with Washington, for instance, ruined him. When he appealed to the public for support against the President by publishing a *Vindication,* moreover, he made his situation worse, for no Secretary, or former Secretary, can compete with the influence of the Presidency, and Randolph could not make a dent in Washington's amazing popularity. In all such cases, where the Secretary has chosen to bring the issue of his differences with the President before the public, the result has been similar. The Secretary has been the loser.

Robert Smith's case illustrates the point. He foolishly sought revenge for his dismissal by publicly attacking President Madison and seeking to overthrow him. Mistakenly, he believed the course he took "will lead to the injury of Mr. Madison and to my advantage." His attack, published as a pamphlet entitled an *Address to the People of the United States,* caused the President much concern, as it did old John Adams, who, seeing in the quarrel a similarity to his difficulties with Timothy Pickering, asked: "Must a President publish a justificatory Proclamation containing all his Reasons, for dismissing a Secretary of State?"

In addition, the feud between Smith and Madison touched off a newspaper battle joined by partisans of both men. The President became so disturbed that he commissioned Joel Barlow, poet and politician, to refute Smith. Barlow publicized Madison's charge that Smith had obtained his appointment through intrigue, that he had long shown a "want of capacity and integrity," and that he was in general unfit for the Secretaryship.

Despite Smith's spirited defense of his conduct, he lost the fight. Because of the nature of the relationship between the President and his Secretary of State, there could have been no other result.

Wishing to avoid a public feud such as Smith precipitated, some Presidents have retained Secretaries with whom they have quarreled. John Adams, for instance, at first hesitated in dismissing the disloyal Pickering because he feared that the removal would arouse "a turbulent session" in Congress and perhaps split his own party. In later years, Pickering defended his conduct as Secretary of State, questioned Adams' motives in removing him, and carried on a debate with Adams over those points. As in the Randolph and Smith cases, Pickering had the weaker side and showed that in an argument with the President, the Secretary has few weapons.

James Buchanan understood this principle well. He accepted his humiliating status under Polk because he realized that if he resigned as a result of a difference with the President, his political career might collapse. Later, when his own Secretary of State, Lewis Cass, resigned on a note of righteous protest because of a difference of opinion with him, Buchanan also learned that in a quarrel with a politically powerful Secretary, a President can expect some discomfort. Cass's friends rallied around him and an aroused Northern public showered abuse on Buchanan. For a while Cass was a popular hero and Buchanan almost a villain. Later, Cass tried to return to the Secretaryship, but Buchanan would have nothing to do with him, and again the President ultimately emerged on top.

Unlike Smith and Cass, William Jennings Bryan knew that his quarrel with Wilson over policy toward Germany would ruin him once his resignation made it public. Such action, a friend pointed out to Mrs. Bryan, "would be bitterly resented by the country; and he would be condemned . . . because the American people would believe that he had resigned for the purpose of embarrassing the President." He told Bryan himself, "I don't want you to destroy yourself."

Bryan replied, "I believe you are right; I think this will destroy me; but whether it does or does not, I must do my duty according to my conscience. . . ." Later, in his last luncheon with the other department heads, he said, "as I leave the Cabinet I go out into the dark . . . the President has the prestige and power on his side."

True enough; Bryan's resignation created a sensation in the press, aroused public opinion against him, and won widespread sympathy for the President. Pro-Allied newspapers and other journals dubbed him mentally incompetent, an unthinking pacifist, a pro-German, and practically a traitor. In his long political career, Bryan had been abused frequently, but never with the viciousness that followed his resignation from the Secretaryship. The general reaction was that the Secretary owed it to his party and country to stand by the President in a time of crisis, that Wilson was right and Bryan wrong. "He was quitting under fire," men said.

The quarrel and resignation broke Bryan's power within the Democratic Party and crushed him personally. With his personal and political popularity gone, his resignation became an ineffective gesture.

Robert Lansing's quarrel with Wilson, on the other hand, did not rally public sentiment behind the President. Wilson had demanded his Secretary's resignation because during Wilson's illness, Lansing had convened the Cabinet without consulting him and, thus, ostensibly had usurped Presidential authority. "It would relieve me of embarrassment, Mr. Secretary," Wilson said, "the embarrassment of feeling your reluctance and divergence of judgment, if you would give up your present office and afford me an opportunity to select some one whose mind would more willingly go along with mine."

When Joseph Tumulty, Wilson's private secretary, first saw this demand, he tried to dissuade the President from sending it, arguing that it would not strike the public in the right way. "Tumulty," Wilson answered with a show of fire, "it is never the wrong time to spike disloyalty. When Lansing sought to oust me, I was upon my back. I am on my feet now and will not have disloyalty about me."

To make matters worse, Wilson published the correspondence between Lansing and himself. That correspondence and the resignation shocked the nation. "It seems," one of Wilson's friends wrote, "the petulant and irritable act of a sick man." Public and press opinion this time sided with the Secretary of State. Many came to regard Lansing as a martyr. It was not the dismissal itself that aroused public sentiment in favor of Lansing, but Wilson's abruptness and the reasons he gave for ridding himself of Lansing.

"My greatest expectations have been more than satisfied," Lansing naïvely confided to his diary. "I never for a moment dreamed of having the whole country rise to my support. I knew that in the exchange of letters I had the better of it, but I did not realize how much the better of it until the people spoke."

Wilson, too, sensed that he had acted hastily. After the initial public reaction to the Lansing resignation, Wilson asked, "Well, Tumulty, have I any friends left?"

"Very few, Governor," Tumulty replied.

Wilson then observed:

. . . in a few days what the country considers an indiscretion on my part in getting rid of Lansing will be forgotten, but when the sober, second thought of the country begins to assert itself, what will stand out will be the disloyalty of Lansing to me. Just think of it! Raised and exalted to the office of Secretary of State, made a member of the Peace Commission, participating in all the conferences and affixing his signature to a solemn treaty, and then hurrying to . . . repudiate the very thing to which he had given his assent.

Although Wilson himself did not come out well in this feud, it is clear that when the furor died, no one could truly question the right of the President to rid himself of a Secretary he disliked. Again, as in the past, the Secretary of State had come out second best in the long run.

The same was true of Byrnes in his feud with Truman. After Byrnes had left office, the President brought the quarrel into the open by allowing a letter of his to Byrnes to be published in which he had accused Byrnes of insubordination while the South Carolinian had held the Secretaryship. Byrnes struck back through an article in *Collier's* magazine in which he denied the charge and asserted that he had never seen the letter until it was published.

Regardless of the merits of the Byrnes case, or of any of the others, the Secretary of State can never gain the attention for his side of the argument that the President can for his. Most Secretaries know this and hence try to keep their differences with the President to themselves, for arguments with the President are never disagreements between equals.

In summary, if the partnership is to work smoothly, the Secretary of State should not arouse any fear in the President that he is being overshadowed; he should not assume powers that belong to the senior partner without the President's sanction; and he should be wise enough to avoid quarreling with his chief. He should keep the President fully and immediately informed on all important matters so that the President has all the freedom of decision a given situation permits in carrying out his Constitutional duty of directing foreign policy. The President, on the other hand, can contribute to the partnership by using his Secretary's advice, whenever appropriate, in shaping policy and by sharing his power in arriving at decisions, though the ultimate decision is always the President's.

7

Statesmanship and Politics

Every Secretary of State, second only to his President, and alone among appointive officers of the Government, stands before the world as the representative of the United States of America. No man who holds this office can fail to feel the extraordinary responsibility he carries for service to the country and its peace. No man has a greater right to ask the sympathetic support and cooperation of his fellow-citizens, and none is more properly exempt from the ordinary trials of politics.
—HENRY L. STIMSON, 1950

IF, over the years, Americans have fashioned a popular image of the Secretary of State, one that sets him apart from other executive officers, it is that he, second only to the President, is a statesman, an official who deals with issues and policies on the highest level. In contrast to other officeholders whom they might class as politicians, the people apparently see the Secretary as a statesman who functions on the level of prime ministers, incorrect though this view may be. They see him as a powerful official responsible for the management of affairs of state, one whose views carry considerable weight in the making of decisions that affect the whole nation, one who is or should be immune from the ordinary stresses of domestic politics.

Yet, historically, the Secretaryship has been as thoroughly meshed into the American political system as any other office in the executive branch and its control has been governed more often by domestic considerations than by concern for broad statesmanship. The popular image and the historical pattern are not contradictory, however, for the office has been hospitable to both the statesman and the politician, and from the beginning men who have taken the office have done so with the idea of becoming statesmen though they may not have been such previously.

When Thomas Jefferson accepted the newly created Secretaryship, for instance, he expressed distaste for its domestic responsibilities and alarm at "the extent of that office, embracing as it does the principal mass of domestic administration, together with the foreign." He wished to be a statesman and hence was assured that as Secretary of State he would not be encumbered with trifling duties.

One of the first to define his own idea of the Secretaryship before he took office and, like Jefferson, to seek assurance that he would be allowed to function as a statesman was James Monroe. He told President Madison that he would join the Administration only if its foreign policy were not so inflexible as to bar his own views from consideration, for he wanted the direction of foreign relations placed in his hands. In effect, he also brought up the issue of whether or not a Secretary and a President, even though of the same political faith, could work together when they held differing views on foreign policy.

"It would not become me to accept a station, and to act a part in it," Monroe explained, "which my judgment and conscience did not approve, and which I did not believe would promote the public welfare and happiness. I could not do this, nor would you wish me to do it. If you are disposed to accept my services under these circumstances and with this explanation, I shall be ready to render them."

Without promising a free hand in foreign policy but nevertheless giving the impression that the new Secretary would be treated as a statesman and enjoy a considerable independence, Madison accepted Monroe's services. "With the mutual knowledge of our respective views of the foreign as well as the domestic interests of our country," the President said, "I see no serious obstacle on either side to an association of our labors in promoting them." Differences of opinion on foreign policy, he added, "must be looked for, even among those most agreed on the same general views. These differences, however, lie fairly within the compass of free consultation and mutual concession as subordinate to the unity belonging to the Executive department."

At first, the Secretary and the President gave the appearance of having overcome their differences. "On public affairs," Monroe wrote, "we confer without reserve, each party expressing his own sentiments, and viewing dispassionately the existing state, animated by a sincere desire to promote the public welfare." Soon, however, the old conflict burst to the surface. Monroe, in effect, urged a policy friendly to Great Britain whereas Madison persisted, seemingly, in favoring France. The President, moreover, tried to keep control of foreign policy in his own hands, refusing to delegate major responsibility to his Secretary.

Monroe, of course, was not happy, particularly with the policy that led to the War of 1812. He explained to an old friend that his Secretaryship was turning out far differently than he and his supporters had expected. "I have been afraid to write to you for some time past," the Secretary said, "because I know that you expected better things from me than I have been able to perform." In fact, he reversed himself. Instead of replacing the President's foreign policy with his own, as he had planned, he found himself not only committed to the President's policy but also to supporting a program he had previously opposed. We can see, therefore, that Monroe was a statesman not in the sense that he was able to shape policy from his own ideas but in the sense that he was able to manage affairs of state planned by others.

John Quincy Adams, the next Secretary of State, took office determined to act the statesman, and also to accept and not to attempt to change the President's policies. In his words:

For myself, I shall enter upon the functions of my office with a deep sense of the necessity of union with my colleagues, and with a suitable impression that my place is *subordinate*. That my duty will be to *support*, and not to counteract or oppose, the President's administration, and that if from any cause I should find my efforts to that end ineffectual, it will be my duty seasonably to withdraw from the public service, and to leave to more competent persons the performance of the duties to which I find myself inadequate.

Adams proved himself a statesman in the best sense of the term. He was able to work closely with the President and through him to make his own ideas policy. He was, in fact, more the statesman in the Secretaryship than in the Presidency.

So great did Adams' reputation as a statesman become that some seventy-five years later, John Hay, another Secretary of State who gave deep thought to the powers and meaning of his office, studied Adams' diary seeking a guiding thread or ideas that would help him to understand the Secretaryship. His search probably was not rewarding, for his conclusions were bitterly negative. "The real duties of a Secretary of State seem to be these," he wrote: "to fight claims upon us by other States; to press more or less fraudulent claims of our citizens upon other countries; to find offices for the friends of Senators where there are none."

One reason for Hay's sour evaluation is that he held an exalted view of the Secretaryship, seeing the Secretary, and hence himself, as a statesman who should not be trammeled by political compromises. Government by experts seems to have been his ideal, a concept that ran counter to the history of his office and for which there was no firm basis in the American tradition. Politics in foreign policy and the functioning of the Secretaryship irked him, and he scathingly denounced those to whom politics provided the meat of statesmanship. In all, Hay had a high sense of the dignity of his office but cherished a distorted ideal of its prerogatives.

So elevated did Hay's view of the Secretaryship become that he came to believe it should be above politics. This can be seen in his reaction when Theodore Roosevelt asked him in the spring of 1904 to speak in New York to aid the Republican campaign there. "It is intolerable," the Secretary wrote in his diary, "that they should not see how much more advantageous to the Administration it is that I should stay at home to do my work than that I should cavort around the country making lean and jejune orations."

Hay eventually agreed to speak, but complained that the Secretary of State should not participate in political campaigns. To do so, he said, would create a bad effect on the diplomatic corps and injure his precarious relations with the Senate. Roosevelt replied bluntly that if Hay would not make a political speech, the election might be lost and then he would no longer be Secretary of State.

In other ways, too, Hay's appraisal of his office was unrealistic. "If a Secretary of State could work in a vacuum," he once told a friend, "and only do the things which would be of advantage to the country, I could imagine no place more delightful than this, but the unconditioned and the absolute are beyond the reach of mortal men, and everything we do must pass the ordeal of a thousand selfish interests and prejudices and spites."

As unrealistic as any of Hay's views was his conviction that the Senate was virtually the natural enemy of the Secretary of State. He hated Congress for its alleged interference in matters of foreign policy, and his writings abound with denunciations of the Senate. The following is typical of his complaints:

> We are so handicapped by the Senate and the House that there is nothing to do but follow a policy of makeshifts and half measures. I see absolutely no chance of any improvement. The President himself is unable to carry out the measures he thinks best. He is unable even to make the appointments he thinks best, and as for the Secretary of State, he is extremely fortunate if he can bring to pass one tenth of the measures for the public good that the Department has elaborated.

So contemptuous of Congress and so concerned with the importance of his office did Hay become that he came to consider it beneath the dignity of the Secretary of State to appear before

Congressional committees. His main concern, however, was the Senate's power over treaties. He once told a friend that "the irreparable mistake of our Constitution puts it into the power of one third + 1 of the Senate to meet with categorical veto any treaty negotiated by the President, even though it may have the approval of nine tenths of the people of the nation." Such bitter complaints, of course, did not make him popular with members of Congress and politicians.

Hay's hatred of the Senate was foolish. He should have realized that a wise Secretary of State does not attempt to reform Congress, but tries instead to learn to live with it, for without reliable support in Congress he usually can accomplish little. This, for instance, was particularly true of Henry Clay. Throughout his term, he and John Quincy Adams had to face a hostile Congress and hence Clay served as a kind of foreign minister to a beleaguered Administration. With anti-Administration forces running Congress, especially the Senate, there was little he could do to carry out Administration policy.

Hay's friend, the historian Henry Adams, lamented this relationship of the Secretary to Congress, saying:

> The Secretary of State has always stood as much alone as the historian. Required to look far ahead and round him, he measures forces unknown to party managers, and has found Congress more or less hostile ever since Congress first sat. The Secretary of State exists only to recognize the existence of a world which Congress would rather ignore; of obligations which Congress repudiates whenever it can; of bargains which Congress distrusts and tries to turn to its advantage or to reject. Since the first day the Senate existed it has always intrigued against the Secretary of State whenever the Secretary has been obliged to extend his functions beyond the appointment of Consuls in Senators' service.

I.

Other critics have maintained that one of the reasons for the Secretary's difficulties with Congress is that he usually has no way of expressing himself politically except through the President. Unlike the foreign secretaries in the parliamentary system, he cannot appear before Congress to explain and defend his policies or even the activities of his department. It is the President who has to defend the Administration's foreign policy. He, not the Secretary of State, reports to Congress and to the people on the state of foreign relations, usually in his regular or special messages on the state of the union.

The Secretary of State reports only to the President; he is the only department head not required by statute, or the traditions of his office, to report or give information regularly to Congress on the policies of his department. This is the President's responsibility. Moreover, if either house of Congress passes a resolution demanding information on foreign relations, the Secretary of State may refuse to comply with it if he deems the release of the information contrary to the "public interest." Congress, therefore, makes its request with the proviso that the release will not endanger the national interest. When the Secretary does forward the information, he does so through the President.

Keen politicians, such as Theodore Roosevelt, realized that they needed the support of Congress for their foreign policies and sought its cooperation. Roosevelt was bothered by Hay's notoriously poor relations with Congress and appointed Elihu Root as his successor at least partly because he thought Root could remedy the difficulty between the State Department and Capitol Hill. During his years in the War Department, Root had learned to get along well with the Senate. "He has managed Congress better than any Cabinet Minister I have known," a friend told the President of Root, "and I know he will manage the Senate better than any Secretary of State I have known."

Roosevelt and his friend were right. Root had become a master in dealing with Congress. To cement cordial relations, he regularly attended meetings of the Senate's Committee on Foreign Relations. "In fact," one Senator remarked, "he became so constant and punctual in his attendance at the meetings of the Committee that we grew almost to regard him as a regular member."

Later, particularly in the years after World War II, the direct contacts between the Secretary of State and Congress on questions of foreign policy increased. As the demands on the President became greater and more complex, the Secretary came to assume the enlarged responsibility of acting as his agent in dealing with Congress on questions of foreign policy. This task required him to use the President's prestige as effectively as possible in gaining support without at the same time downgrading his own status.

The Secretary and his staff now appeared before various Congressional committees to explain, defend, or plead for Administration policies. At times, the Secretary even conferred with the Senate Committee on Foreign Relations in advance of important diplomatic negotiations. This seemed a wise procedure, since under the committee system in Congress, committee assent, particularly in the case of a treaty, was tantamount to Senate approval if the matter were negotiated as the committee desired.

When seeking support for a treaty or for particular legislation, the Secretary of State now at times went before Congressional committees at his own request. Usually, however, Congress asked him to appear. In the years of the Cold War, Congress came to take a greater interest than before in foreign affairs and members of both houses, usually in committees, sought to be "briefed" on international developments by the Secretary himself. Sometimes the Secretary testified before the committees in executive session, where he could speak freely and frankly present his case. When, however, he appeared before public sessions, he could not speak with the freedom he might desire.

The Franklin D. Roosevelt, Truman, Eisenhower, and Kennedy Administrations have all considered close liaison with Congress so important that the Department of State assigned one of its ranking officers the task of maintaining that liaison. Still, the Secretary's relations with Congress have not been smooth, or, as Acheson's and Dulles' Secretaryships show, even cordial. The nature of the Secretaryship, virtually independent of Congressional control, is in part responsible for this.

At the same time, though he usually has no independent political influence, the Secretary, as the President's agent, is a political official whom the men in Congress can attack or defend as they would any political appointee. Few Secretaries, moreover, had extensive Congressional experience and hence many of them could not fully understand or gain the confidence of Congress. Furthermore, a Secretary can seldom separate his Administration's politics from foreign policy.

In trying to maintain cordial relations with Congress, actually in attempting to bridge the gap in part created by the separation of powers, the Secretary of State has had a checkered experience. Until the change of recent years, he usually approached Congress directly only through committees dealing with legislative matters concerning his department, mainly the foreign-affairs committees of both houses. Only as the appropriations committees came to deal with his own budget did the Secretary appear before them. After World War II, when economic foreign policy became critically important, the appropriations committees became virtually his regular channels of communication with Congress. At the same time, Congress' expanded participation in foreign affairs made it imperative that he be concerned with the activities of some of the committees that seemed thoroughly domestic in their work, such as those on agriculture. Actually, the disposal of enormous farm surpluses abroad, often the result of Congressional action, certainly has an impact on foreign relations.

Dulles' record illustrates the increased demand of the Congressional committees on the Secretary's time. In his first three years in office, he met with committees or subcommittees of Congress one hundred and twenty times. From 1955 to 1958, he met on an average of six to eight times a month with important Senators and Congressmen, and two or three times with representatives from foreign-affairs, appropriations, and other committees. When Congress was in session, he appeared before its various committees concerned with foreign affairs about six times a month, and some months as often as twelve times.

Dulles also attended some of the occasional conferences that the President had with leaders from both houses, meetings that have now become almost an established practice. In time of crisis in foreign relations, the President has met with Congressional leaders on what has appeared to be almost a regular schedule, often on a weekly basis. A wise President would do well, whenever possible, to have his Secretary of State at his side during these conferences.

Never, until Cordell Hull's time, however, did a Secretary of State appear before the whole Congress to make a personal report. Hull's speech before a joint session of Congress in November, 1944, after his return from a conference in Moscow, was unprecedented. It reflected his unique personal influence upon Congress.

Although he lacked Hull's political background, Dean Acheson went as far as any Secretary of State in trying to build good relations with Congress. He experimented with an unofficial conference with members of Congress for the purpose of answering questions on the Administration's foreign policy. After speaking to an informal joint session of Congress in the Coolidge Auditorium of the Library of Congress, he submitted to an unprecedented questioning. This unusual experiment was ostensibly to bring Congress into the making of foreign policy and make it possible for the Secretary and Congress to meet on neutral ground, but it failed. Since Acheson was himself under fire from Congressional critics, he could not remove the Secretaryship from political warfare.

Acheson's and Dulles' difficulties with Congress led some political analysts to contend that a Secretary of State must have political experience to be effective. Only with political influence in his own right, such as Hull or Herter had, they have said, can a Secretary conduct foreign relations free from political attacks at home. Without such support, the argument goes, a Secretary cannot fully meet the demands of his office.

This argument, of course, runs counter to John Hay's idea, one shared by Henry L. Stimson, that the Secretary of State should be above politics. In 1932, President Hoover collided with this idea when he asked Stimson to make a speech attacking Franklin

D. Roosevelt, the Democratic candidate for President. The Secretary refused, saying "he considered such partisan polemics
improper in a Secretary of State." He maintained that "to use
the great office of Secretary of State to launch a purely personal
attack on Roosevelt is quite inconsistent with my dignity and
that of the office." Stimson, who had at one time also been
Secretary of War, believed that the Secretaryship of State was
"the most nonpartisan in the Cabinet."

Hoover disagreed with his Secretary's view. "Secretary Stimson
who had taken part in Republican political campaigns for many
years past," he wrote, "felt that he must, as Secretary of State,
be neutral. He was the first Cabinet leader in history to take that
view."

Although mistaken in detail, Hoover was right in principle.
Stimson's idea of a nonpartisan Secretary has no strong historical
foundation. The refusal of a Secretary of State to campaign for
his President, in fact, contradicts one of the traditional rules
governing his selection. Presidents have generally expected their
Secretaries to bring them political strength and, at times, have
even retained Secretaries they did not want because they desired the support those Secretaries could give the Administration.

Seward's national prestige and high status within the Republican Party were assets that Lincoln wanted and needed.
Andrew Johnson, in turn, retained Seward in the Secretaryship
because he wished to identify his Administration and his Reconstruction problems with plans bequeathed by Lincoln. Seward,
who had been a vital instrument in the Lincoln policies, fur-
thered that identification. In other words, he was able to bring
Johnson political support.

Years later, Theodore Roosevelt kept John Hay, even though
he preferred a new Secretary of his own choice, because "his
name, his reputation, his staunch loyalty, all made him a real
asset of the administration."

Similarly, Wilson needed Bryan in the Secretaryship primarily
for the political strength the Great Commoner could bring to his
domestic program. Bryan's support, for instance, proved in-

valuable in obtaining Congressional approval for the Federal Reserve Act.

Bryan's successor even hesitated in accepting the Secretaryship because he lacked political influence. "Such influence," Lansing wrote, "was and is an important qualification for a Cabinet officer in carrying through a general legislative program, a fact which had been proved by Bryan during his two years as Secretary, and without which some of the important legislation sought by the President would undoubtedly have failed." Bryan's tenure thus illustrates that a politically powerful Secretary of State can be an asset in a way that a nonpartisan Secretary, if there has ever truly been one, can never be.

This principle can also be seen at work in the case of Cordell Hull. With him at the head of the Cabinet, Roosevelt could keep Congress, mainly the Southern Democrats there, loyal to his Administration and its policies.

Hull frequently threatened to resign, particularly when he heard that one of his subordinates was attempting to evade his authority with "backstairs business" at the White House. Harry Hopkins got so tired of Hull's periodic threats that he hoped that the President would someday accept the Secretary's offer to resign, but Roosevelt never did. In a showdown, in fact, he invariably supported his Secretary of State.

For instance, though Roosevelt preferred Sumner Welles to Hull in the handling of foreign affairs, in 1943 when the feud between the two men became so intense that he had to choose between them, he sided with Hull. Political influence won out over his own desire.

Roosevelt could never forget Wilson's crushing experience with the Senate a quarter of a century earlier, when the League of Nations was defeated. He realized that he would need Hull's potent influence in gaining the Senate's approval for postwar treaties, and if he should seek re-election in the following year. Hull, moreover, was one of the most popular members of the Administration, one who had a following of his own. Rather than risk the loss of any kind of political support that Hull could give him, Roosevelt reluctantly let Welles go.

Like some of his predecessors, furthermore, Roosevelt dreaded the political repercussions likely to flow from Hull's resignation, even though he could have weathered the tempest. A number of Presidents, Polk, for example, have retained Secretaries they did not want because they feared the political reaction of a removal. So valuable a political asset did Roosevelt consider Hull, in fact, that in October, 1944, when the Secretary said he must resign, the President persuaded him to withhold the resignation until after the November elections. He did not wish to lose Hull's prestige in the midst of his fourth-term battle. Few Presidents understood the importance of a politically influential Secretary of State as well as did Roosevelt and probably none used him as effectively in obtaining support for Administration policies.

Despite his independent influence and popularity, Hull was not a powerful Secretary of State. His Secretaryship, therefore, contradicts the conviction held by some politicians that, to be truly successful, a Secretary must be popular. Seward's political mentor, Thurlow Weed, for example, told him, "In the position you are to assume all the qualities that won men and made you popular are required. To be successful you must be a popular Secretary. And this popularity depends largely upon manner and temper."

II.

Seward was not a popular Secretary of State; neither was Acheson or Dulles. Yet all three, in the sense that they were statesmen who shaped foreign policy, were more powerful and hence more successful than Hull. All three suffered slander and vilification from political opponents. One reason for Acheson's difficulties— a factor beyond his power to control—was that he, more than any other person in the second Truman Administration, came to symbolize American foreign policy. Those who hated that policy, or the Administration itself, attacked him, for unlike Hull, he had few defenders in Congress. Since he had no independent following, even within his own party, he became a practically defenseless prey for those legislators hunting for political issues.

Acheson's troubles also stemmed from the fact that during his time, the early years of the Cold War, the Secretaryship came to assume greater importance, at home and throughout the world, than ever before. People had a vague idea that perhaps he might be the cause of difficulty in uncertain times and some blamed him for the President's policies. Unlike the President, or the men of Congress, but like his predecessors, he was not under constant surveillance by reporters. The reporters, and consequently the people, saw him only occasionally, and when they did, as in his press conferences, he usually delivered prepared statements and occasionally seemed condescending.

By the very nature of his office and the vagueness of his powers, the Secretary of State may give the impression of being a mysterious figure, one who invites suspicion, mainly it seems, because he appears at times not sufficiently ardent in his defense of "national" policies against foreign interests. Sometimes if, like Hull, a Secretary has a good press or a strong political following, he may even receive credit for accomplishments that are not his own. If he has neither, as in the case of Acheson, people may blame him for policies or blunders that are not his own. Then, as they did with Acheson, politicians can use the Secretary of State as a scapegoat for policies they do not like.

Acheson was never able to popularize himself or to achieve a respected status with the masses or the politicians. His predicament seems to demonstrate that a Secretary of State without political support, no matter how well qualified in the conduct of foreign affairs, in a time of intensified and frustrated concern over foreign policy, faces grave difficulties at the hands of politicians. The Secretary's helplessness in the face of Congressional attacks is in part imbedded in the American political system and in the structure of his office. He does not have at his own disposal, as do the President and other department heads, the usual political weapons of reward and reprisal with which to blunt Congressional opposition or to gain Congressional support.

More than any other, the politician who attempted to take advantage of the national frustration over foreign policy during the early days of the Cold War was Senator Joseph R. McCarthy, a Republican from Wisconsin who touched off a debate on the political complexion of the State Department in February, 1950, by charging that it was honeycombed with Communists. Before he was through, McCarthy was able to make the character of the Secretary of State himself a foremost political issue.

The Senate held long hearings on McCarthy's charges against Acheson and his department and, despite the fact that no evidence of disloyalty was uncovered, the gunning for the Secretary continued until he went out of office. "The charges against him had no foundation whatever," a prominent Senator wrote, "but unfortunately they served to undermine the administration's foreign policy and to gain publicity for Acheson's critics."

Although few voices, in Congress and elsewhere, rose to Acheson's defense, he did have some defenders, among them Henry L. Stimson. Although almost at the point of death, Stimson expressed resentment and alarm over the attacks on the Secretaryship. "It seems quite clear that the real motive of the accuser in this case is to cast discredit upon the Secretary of State of the United States," he said. And, he added, "In any test of personal confidence the men of honor, in both parties, will choose to stand with the Secretary."

The Secretary of State, he pointed out, has the right to expect the sympathy and support of the people, and then referred to an old idea, that the Secretary should be exempt from the ordinary trials of politics. "The man who seeks to gain political advantage from personal attack on a Secretary of State," he declared, "is a man who seeks political advantage from damage to his country." At that time, however, Stimson's voice was that of a minority, for the campaign against Acheson continued, leading to demands for his resignation.

"The blunt fact is," a newspaper editorial said, "the most important post in Mr. Truman's administration is filled by a man who does not enjoy general or congressional confidence." Even a former Cabinet colleague, Harold L. Ickes, demanded Acheson's resignation. "I will go further," he said of the editorial, "and affirm that, on the basis of knowledge that I possess, he does not 'enjoy the confidence' of many who are prominent colleagues of his in the Administration, to say nothing of Democratic political leaders throughout the country."

Finally, the attacks against his Secretary of State so angered Truman that he lashed out in defense of Acheson. "How our position in the world would be improved by the retirement of Dean Acheson from public life," he said, "is beyond me." He insisted that the charges were false and pointed out that Seward had suffered from similar slander. As Lincoln refused to dismiss Seward, the President announced, "so do I refuse to dismiss Secretary Acheson."

Later Truman wrote that "the men who struck out against Acheson were thus in reality striking out at me." He was right, for since the Secretary technically has no personal responsibility for policy and is the spokesman for the President's policy, it is almost axiomatic that one way to attack the President is through his Secretary of State. "In other words," Truman said, "they wanted Acheson's scalp because he stood for *my* policy."

Acheson's tenure spanned a period when the opposition party attacked Administration foreign policy, and hence the Secretary of State, as savagely as any policy or Secretary has ever been attacked. Acheson himself wrote that "in 1950–52 the ferocity of the Republican attack knew no limits." Nonetheless, Acheson was not driven from office, and thus he gave strength to the principle that if a President stands by his Secretary and chooses to support him in the face of partisan political onslaughts, the Secretary of State can withstand almost any kind of pressure or criticism.

This principle can also be seen at work in the case of John Foster Dulles. Acheson, at least, was admired abroad, but Dulles was distrusted not only by the opposition party but also by his country's allies. In England, one member of Parliament attacked him, perhaps unjustly, saying that never before had a man "spent so long in preparing himself to be Foreign Secretary and made such a fool of himself when he finally got the job." At home, Democrats disliked him, particularly for his inconsistencies and apparent efforts to wring political advantage from foreign policy.

The most powerful attacks on Dulles came after the Suez crisis of 1956, which nearly ruined America's Middle Eastern policy and her alliance with Great Britain and France. The British and French, who had invaded Egypt and were forced to withdraw in part because of American pressure, felt that Dulles had betrayed them. Friends as well as critics, therefore, pointed out that a Secretary of State who is distrusted by his country's major allies cannot be effective. "How long," one newspaper asked, "can the United States afford the luxury of a Secretary of State in whom there is so little confidence at home and abroad?"

By this time, the Secretary had succeeded in alienating nearly the whole Democratic Party in Congress. Even some influential members of Dulles' own party shared this lack of confidence in him, though Republicans rallied to his defense as Democrats in Congress had not to that of Acheson. More important, Eisenhower stood by his Secretary's side just as Truman had rushed to the defense of Acheson. The President made it clear that he wholeheartedly supported Dulles and was responsible for his policies, which, he said, "have my approval from top to bottom."

Some observers, remembering Acheson's ordeal, now concluded that the bitterness between Congress and the Secretary of State in a time of international tension is not unusual. It is almost inevitable, they said, because the Secretary cannot avoid dealing with Congress in his role as a representative and even defender of the Administration in power. He frequently does not have the luxury of choosing between a partisan or bipartisan approach to Congress.

Students of government have also pointed out that the new controversial and intense concern with foreign affairs makes it practically impossible for a Secretary of State to be popular and still do his job well. James F. Byrnes, in contrast to Thurlow Weed almost a century earlier, stated that "one of the functions of a good Secretary of State is to be unpopular," for the Secretary has become a symbol and personification of the international frustrations that Americans could not escape or resolve. The fact that the Secretary offers a ready target for the pent-up anger produced by these frustrations, it was said, is merely one of the unpleasant occupational hazards of the modern Secretaryship.

Although it is true that some of Dulles' difficulties seem inherent in the problems he had to face, he also created certain of his own handicaps. Despite a formal espousal of bipartisanism in foreign policy, he was himself as Secretary of State a narrow partisan. He paid close attention to the needs of the Republican Party in foreign affairs and seldom hesitated to blame Democrats for some of his predicaments. His partisanship, however, was not merely a personal trait. It reflected the times. The new controversy over the nature of foreign policy made the Secretary of State a partisan to a degree that had no clear historical precedent. Indeed, as one political writer pointed out, at times the main issue in foreign policy between the Democrats and Dulles seemed to be Dulles himself.

Dulles, moreover, seems to have had a knack for plunging into controversy. Critics quipped that he was born with a silver hoof in his mouth. One source of controversy stemmed from his conviction that foreign policy begins at home and should be based on domestic political considerations, on what he called the realities of American politics. When domestic and international considerations clashed, his theory held, domestic politics should take precedence. This attitude led to compromises with hectoring politicians, such as Senator McCarthy, who continued to attack the State Department even though it was now controlled by his own party.

Dulles' concern for domestic political support grew out of his determination, among other things, not to repeat Acheson's failure to gain the support of Congress and of the press, just as Acheson had been determined not to repeat Byrnes's failure to hold the President's confidence. Despite his precautions, Dulles failed. In many ways, he had a less favorable press than Acheson and though his record of getting along with Congress was at first better than Acheson's, it too was poor. He seems to have had a passion not to offend Congress, and yet did. Only Eisenhower's popularity saved Dulles from any harsher criticism than he received.

As a general rule, opposition to a Secretary of State is just another means of attacking the President, but Eisenhower was so popular that few politicians openly attacked him or attempted to force his Secretary from office. His second Secretary, Christian A. Herter, offered no problem. Having served several terms in the House of Representatives, Herter had many friends in Congress. He was, in fact, one of the most popular men to take over the Secretaryship. His popularity and political record probably saved him from Congressional flailings for several blunders, notably for his part in the U-2 fiasco and in Japan's humiliating last-minute cancellation of Eisenhower's visit to Tokyo in the summer of 1960.

More than a century earlier, those who mercilessly attacked John M. Clayton, thinking he ran the Administration, did so to strike at President Zachary Taylor, even though, like Eisenhower, he took office as a war hero. Clayton's seventeen months in the Secretaryship, therefore, were unhappy. Unpopular and subjected to savage criticism for policies that were not his own, he was politically helpless, having no official means, no political influence of his own, that he could invoke to defend himself or Administration foreign policy. That defense had to come from the President himself. All Clayton could do was to absorb the criticisms or act as a shield for the President.

When Taylor died in office, despite his grief over the personal loss, Clayton was grateful for the opportunity to resign gracefully. "The situation I have filled," he wrote, "was during the period of President Taylor's administration more difficult, more thorny and more liable to misrepresentation and calumny than any other in the world, as I verily believe."

his own authority was clear and unencumbered. In effect, they provided for strengthening the Secretary's role of statesman by enlarging his power over the formulating of policy. After considering the Hoover Commission's report, Congress passed a law in May, 1949, that confirmed and enlarged the Secretary's authority over policy and freed him from certain routine administrative duties by giving him additional assistant secretaries.

Despite this concern for statesmanship, the history of the Secretaryship shows that a Secretary of State to be effective must be a politician as well as a statesman. In fact, it is difficult to draw a line between the two. The Secretary cannot work in a sphere of foreign affairs isolated from political developments at home, for the conduct of foreign relations requires political leadership of Congress as well as statesmanship. In the years of the Cold War, moreover, when the Secretary is the center of public attention as he has never been before, his personal and political ideas have attained unprecedented public importance. Many have come to recognize that he is a politician as well as a statesman.

It is as a statesman, nonetheless, and not as a politician, that the Secretary of State usually appears before the American people and the world. If he is to fill that role properly, he should be allowed the power to make decisions, and he must make them; he cannot be content merely to transmit to the President the views and raw ideas of his subordinates. He should use the experts in his department to inform him and stimulate him, but he himself ought to put together the pieces that go into the making of policy. In fact, he should draw on other departments and agencies, as well, for support, information, and ideas. From this unique wide-ranging position that cuts across departmental lines in the hierarchy of government, he has to arrive at his own conclusions and make his own synthesis in formulating the advice he offers the President. When he can persuade the President to use this advice as the basis for action, and when he receives a mandate to carry out the decisions thus arrived at as national policy, the Secretary functions as a statesman in the true meaning of the term in the American system.

8

The Administrator and Diplomat

> As a maker and executor of foreign policy, whatever the appearances, the Secretary of State is not an individual performer. He is part of an institution, another essential part of which is the personnel of the Department of State and the Foreign Service, from which flow to him his initial analyses of problems and recommendations for dealing with them.
> —DEAN G. ACHESON, 1955

LIKE the other members of the Cabinet, the Secretary of State is the head of an institution—in his case, the Department of State—which forms the foundation of his office. This institution acts in his name and feeds him most of the information and recommendations on which he usually bases his own advice to the President. The Secretary, therefore, functions not only as an individual, but also as part of an organization, as an administrator.

Until the sudden expansion of the State Department during World War II, the Secretary's administrative problem, despite the complaints of various Secretaries about their heavy administrative loads, was not truly acute. Now, however, it is imperative that the Secretary be enough of an administrator to control and use his vastly expanded department effectively.

Despite the considerable technical skill that administration may require and the large amount of time that it may absorb, no Secretary of State has achieved a lasting reputation for concentrating on efficiency in administrative detail and departmental routine. Secretaries such as Louis McLane, John Forsyth, and

Edward R. Stettinius, Jr., who carried out major administrative reorganizations within the Department of State, are scarcely remembered, except perhaps by academicians specializing in American diplomacy.

Even so capable a statesman as John Quincy Adams, in a day when the State Department's administrative responsibilities were light, felt despair over the pressing nature of his own daily administrative duties, fearing they would so overwhelm him that he would be able to leave behind him no record of substantial accomplishment in the Secretaryship. Administrative changes, such as one in 1823 that made the Secretary responsible for granting passports to Americans who wished to visit foreign countries, merely added to his burden. Few Secretaries, in fact, have been content to act merely as administrators, and virtually all have considered themselves something more.

Henry Clay, Adams' successor, for instance, detested his administrative responsibilities. In his day, the Department of State was still little more than a collection of clerks, and most of the routine tasks that required decisions fell to the Secretary of State. In retrospect, in part because he clashed with President Adams over policy and appointments, but more because of the administrative duties that bored him, Clay could say that his Secretaryship gave him four of the most miserable and uninteresting years of his life.

Clay's experience, though extreme, is not unusual, for some Presidents, such as Polk, wanted nothing more than administrators as Secretaries of State, men who were capable of handling routine matters on their own but who would not shape policy. "As long as he will carry out my policy and act faithfully," Polk said of Secretary Buchanan, for instance, "I am willing he shall remain in the office of Secretary of State; when he ceases to do so, he must cease to occupy that position."

A quarter of a century later, William L. Evarts thought so little of his administrative duties that he ignored them or left them almost entirely to his subordinates in the State Department. Once, when the President questioned his neglect of administrative matters, Evarts replied, "You don't sufficiently realize the great truth that almost any question will settle itself if you only leave it alone long enough." So lightly did he take his responsibilities that he continued to practice law while in the Secretaryship. Even friends criticized him for this cavalier attitude toward his office. Hamilton Fish, for example, complained that shortly after Evarts took office, before he had had time to acquaint himself with his new responsibilities, he rushed off to New York to plead cases.

Another who accepted outside employment while in the Secretaryship and therefore pushed aside administrative duties, but who also came to feel the lash of savage criticism, was William Jennings Bryan. As he had done for years, Bryan while in office continued to give lectures for pay. In the summer of 1913, while on the Chautauqua circuit, for example, he gave speeches in West Virginia, Maryland, Pennsylvania, and other states. To critics, particularly in the Eastern press, the Secretary of State had "disgraced his office" by stripping it of proper dignity and had descended to the level of a mere entertainer, "a barnstormer, playing one-night stands, preceded by the magic lantern and followed by the hurdy-gurdy man and his dancing bear." Although unprepared for such humiliating attacks, Bryan shrugged them off as best he could and went on with the lectures, for the controversial publicity pulled in larger crowds than before.

Bryan explained that he could not live on the Secretary of State's annual salary of $12,000 and had to lecture for additional income. "Mr. Bryan's attitude in this matter," one critic wrote, "is fundamentally wrong. If a Cabinet officer cannot live on his salary, and is unwilling to use his private means to make up the difference, he has no business to retain the office an instant."

Foreigners, too, joined the criticism. "It is a pity," the British Ambassador wrote, "that Bryan has given so much occasion for Europe to ridicule the State Department. He has, after all, attended to business more in the intervals of his lecturing and golf than Knox did in the intervals of his touring and golf. . . ."

Philander C. Knox, incidentally, detested the administrative duties of the Secretaryship and whenever possible shunned them. He wished to deal only with high policy, not with routine or technical matters. It was probably this attitude that persuaded President Taft that his Secretary of State was lazy. Yet, under Knox, the State Department went through its most thorough reorganization since that carried out by Hamilton Fish in 1870.

John Hay, too, disliked administrative tasks and complained constantly of being overworked. At the end of a year in the Secretaryship, he wrote that "it is impossible to exaggerate the petty worries and cares which, added to the really important matters, make the office of Secretary of State almost intolerable." At another time, he said that "the worst of my present job is that I can delegate so little of it."

Hay did exaggerate his plight, for he was able to delegate administrative responsibilities, relying heavily on Alvey A. Adee, his Second Assistant Secretary of State, who had been in the State Department for twenty-one years and understood virtually every detail of administrative and diplomatic procedure. Adee, a bachelor who would work at night and sleep in his office when the department's work load could not be handled in a normal day, drafted instructions, went through the morning mail, signed official correspondence, and performed other administrative duties. He served until 1924, when he died in harness at the age of eighty-two. Altogether, he had spent forty-seven years in the State Department, easing the administrative burden of twenty-two Secretaries of State.

In fact, it is the work of men such as Adee that has given administrative management in the department an essential continuity. William Hunter, Adee, and Wilbur J. Carr, administrative assistants for various Secretaries of State, served without a break from 1829 to 1937, a period of more than a century. They were professionals whose knowledge of administrative procedures made the problem of administration a manageable one for all Secretaries, regardless of party or policy.

Hay's successor, Elihu Root, who apparently liked administrative tasks and is remembered as a capable administrator, by practical standards was not a sound one because he himself took on too much of the routine work that might better have been delegated to reliable subordinates such as Adee. By the same criteria, Frank B. Kellogg's concern for petty details, his truculent attitude and bursts of temper, which earned him the nickname "nervous Nellie," made him a poor administrator.

Some men have seemed concerned mainly with their administrative responsibilities and have served in the tradition that the Secretary of State is the President's personal administrative officer in foreign affairs. Frederick T. Frelinghuysen, for instance, seems to have considered himself the head of an organization staffed by competent subordinates, the holder of an office that ran itself and required little of him. Others, such as John W. Foster and William R. Day, also apparently considered themselves mainly administrators.

Few Secretaries of State, however, have been as concerned with effective administration as was Charles E. Hughes. His thinking helped to inspire the Rogers Act of 1924, which improved the diplomatic service through salary increases, the merging of the diplomatic and consular services, and the basing of appointments and promotions on merit. "You will find, I believe," he told his successor, "that the Department is more effectively organized than it has ever been."

Cordell Hull took administrative problems seriously. He immersed himself in the mass of routine data that flowed through the State Department, but he cannot be called an able administrator, in part because he accustomed himself to the department's bureaucracy instead of mastering it.

Edward R. Stettinius, Jr., was essentially an administrator, experienced in the management of large corporations. His successor, James F. Byrnes, on the other hand, looked upon administrative obligations as barriers to the Secretary's true responsibilities, believing that the Secretary should be free of purely administrative duties so that he could concentrate on the making of policy. "The amount of time a Secretary of State must give to decisions on carrying out operating functions," he said, "necessarily is taken away from the important questions of foreign policy."

The next Secretary, George C. Marshall, had a deep interest in efficient administration, having been Chief of Staff in control of the nation's military establishment in a time of unparalleled growth. In one of his first chores as Secretary of State, therefore, he reorganized the top command in the State Department so as to clarify the lines of authority. As he had in the army, he entrusted almost all administrative problems to subordinates, to what he called his staff. Like an army commander, furthermore, he demanded orderly staff procedure and kept himself remote from the workings of the department. Under Secretary of State Dean Acheson functioned as his chief of staff and ran the department. Only major questions were submitted to Marshall for decision.

In the War Department, Marshall had been concerned with long-term, centralized planning, which he felt the State Department lacked. Therefore, he created the Policy Planning Staff, a small group of specialists who would work directly under him but outside the usual departmental hierarchy. That group would analyze trends in foreign affairs from the point of view of the Secretary of State's world-wide responsibilities and formulate policy recommendations for some twenty-five years into the future for his guidance and for others who must make the decisions. Under Marshall, perhaps more than under any other Secretary, policy emerged from staff planning. Critics thought he was excessively influenced by his staff, a captive of his own administrative devices.

Like Marshall, Dean Acheson, too, relied heavily on his staff for assistance in formulating policy and administering the State Department, but by experience, he was better qualified than Marshall had been to run the department. Probably no Secretary, in fact, has been as well prepared as an administrator upon taking office as was Acheson. He had served in the State Department continuously for six and a half years, worked under four Secretaries of State and two Presidents, and, as Vice-Chairman of the

Hoover Commission, studied the department. Under Marshall, he had actually administered the department and, moreover, is the only Secretary who was both an Assistant Secretary and an Under Secretary. He knew the internal workings of the department as no other Secretary has.

One of Acheson's first moves as Secretary of State was to carry out a partial reorganization of the State Department along lines recommended by the Hoover Commission. Among other changes, the reorganization relieved the Secretary of some of his administrative responsibilities, for his duties had become so complicated that at times he could be little more than an administrator.

When Dulles was offered the Secretaryship to replace Acheson, he expressed distaste for the Secretary's administrative obligations, saying that he doubted that any Secretary would have time to think clearly if he were to try to administer the State Department and to meet the other routine demands of his office. When he took office, therefore, he indicated that he intended to confine his attention to large issues of policy while leaving the details of administration to subordinates. That was why almost the first piece of legislation President Eisenhower requested of Congress was authorization for two Under Secretaries of State instead of one. Dulles asked for this change because he wanted the second Under Secretary to handle administrative details within the State Department so that he himself could devote most of his time to diplomacy and the making of policy.

Like Stimson, moreover, Dulles virtually ignored the career men in the Department of State and the Foreign Service. Although he delegated administrative responsibilities, he did not do so when such matters touched the making of policy. In fact, he rarely accepted advice from his subordinates and, unlike Acheson, seldom used the Policy Planning Staff. His thinking alone, he appeared to assume, generated foreign policy. As a consequence, he was never popular with his subordinates, most of whom considered him a poor administrator. In contrast, Herter, who tried to give the top officials in the State Department a share in formulating foreign policy, was admired by his subordinates for being a team worker.

I.

Popularity within the State Department and effective administration, however, have had little effect on the reputation of a Secretary of State. Even political power and achievements in domestic affairs, unless they led to the Presidency, have brought no lasting recognition. Those who stand out are the Secretaries who made notable records in the conduct of foreign relations, mainly the diplomats who were also statesmen. Even the lesser figures have gained recognition for their connection to some special idea, to some doctrine, and most of all, to some noteworthy achievement in diplomacy. Such achievement has usually so firmly captured public imagination or so overshadowed all else in a Secretary's tenure as to stamp him with an enduring distinction.

The list of such Secretaries and their accomplishments is long, but a brief mention might refresh faded memories and should illustrate the point. Few can think of the Monroe Doctrine and the Transcontinental Treaty of 1819, which reinforced the claim of the United States to a foothold on the Pacific and took Florida from Spain, without bringing to mind John Quincy Adams, or of the Webster-Ashburton Treaty of 1842, which settled the Maine-boundary dispute with Great Britain, without recalling Daniel Webster. Seward's name is forever linked to the skillful diplomacy of the Civil War and to the purchase of Alaska, Hamilton Fish to the Treaty of Washington in 1871, which settled a number of grievances with England and Canada, Blaine to Pan-Americanism, John Hay to the Open Door Policy, Olney to an extravagant expansion of the Monroe Doctrine related to a boundary dispute between Venezuela and British Guiana, Knox to Dollar Diplomacy, or economic expansion in Asia and Latin America, and Hughes to the Washington Disarmament Conference of 1921–22 which temporarily eased tense relations with Japan.

Kellogg gave his name to the Kellogg-Briand Antiwar Pact and received the Nobel Peace Prize for his part in it. Stimson is best remembered for the nonrecognition doctrine that bears his name and Cordell Hull for his Reciprocal Trade Agreements Program and his work in the founding of the United Nations— a task that earned him a Nobel Peace Prize. George Marshall, too, won a Nobel Peace Prize, mainly for his part in the European Recovery Program, also known as the Marshall Plan. Acheson is noted for his work on the North Atlantic Treaty and for the diplomacy of the Korean War, and Dulles for the idea of "deterrence" and the building of a world-wide network of alliances, one of which is the Southeast Asia Treaty Organization, or SEATO.

We can see, therefore, why the popular image of the Secretary of State is that of a statesman, at least in the sense of being the nation's foremost diplomat. It has not been, however, a constant image. Until the twentieth century, the Secretary conducted practically all his own diplomacy, or personal negotiations, quietly in the United States. In 1791, Thomas Jefferson and the first British Minister to the United States negotiated in Philadelphia for the removal of the British from posts they occupied in the Northwest; later, John Quincy Adams and Spain's Luis de Onís bargained for Florida in Washington, and Seward obtained Alaska from the Russians in a treaty signed in Washington. When, as in the case of the Jay treaty of 1794 with Britain or the Louisiana Purchase, negotiations had to be carried on abroad, the Secretary stayed at home and sent special commissioners to conclude the agreements. In those instances, the special emissaries, not the Secretary, captured whatever glory the negotiations offered.

In the twentieth century, the Secretary of State has become a traveling negotiator, a diplomat on the move. Unless the President himself takes over, the Secretary participates in almost every important negotiation or international conference affecting the United States, no matter where it might be. Using fast ships and streaking airplanes, he has established a new pattern of secretarial conduct.

Lansing attended the Paris Peace Conference, in 1919, Kellogg went to Paris to sign his antiwar treaty, and Stimson went to the Naval Disarmament Conference in London in 1930 and participated in other negotiations abroad. Within a few months of taking office, Cordell Hull headed the American delegation to the World Economic Conference in London and several months later led a delegation to an International Conference of American States in Montevideo. In 1943, even though he had never set foot in an airplane, was seventy-two years old, sick, and suffered from claustrophobia, he was so determined not to be excluded from another major international conference that he suppressed lifelong fears and insisted on making a long arduous flight to Moscow for a conference. The results, he felt, were worth the danger, for at Moscow he obtained the Four-Nation Declaration, signed by the United States, Russia, Great Britain, and China, which laid the basis for the United Nations and gave him his greatest personal triumph as Secretary of State.

The next Secretary, Stettinius, held office only seven months but spent more than half of that time away from the Department of State participating in various international conferences or negotiations. Such extensive travel now began to alarm some students of government, who argued that the Secretary had to concentrate so much on negotiation that he was forced to neglect his administrative and political responsibilities, but more important, he had no time to participate in the making of policy.

While traveling, despite the advanced technology of rapid communication, critics pointed out, the Secretary of State could not keep in close touch with the developments in Washington that went into the shaping of policy. He could not be in a position to make important decisions on the basis of seeing and weighing all the evidence, nor could he make an effective case with the President against competing agencies that had a part in molding foreign policy. This peripatetic diplomacy, some analysts argued on the other hand, merely reflects the President's traditional dominance of foreign policy and the use of the Secretary as his personal agent. One powerful Senator, for instance, called Stettinius "the presidential messenger."

No one could rightly accuse the next Secretary, James F. Byrnes, of being merely a Presidential messenger, yet three days after taking office, he had packed his bags for a "summit" conference at Potsdam. He, too, had no time to take part in the collective policy-making in the Cabinet, for he kept up a fast pace of travel, being away from the State Department conducting negotiations with foreign powers some 62 per cent of the time he held office, or 350 out of 562 days.

George Marshall, Byrnes's successor, followed a similar pattern, spending most of his time as Secretary abroad attending conferences or negotiating with foreign statesmen in the United States. Almost as soon as he took office, he had to prepare himself for a meeting with Russian, British, and French foreign ministers in Moscow. Up to October 15, 1948, he had devoted 228 days out of 633 in office to the diplomacy of international conferences.

Dean Acheson, too, had to commit himself to a schedule of travel and negotiation, but John Foster Dulles, more than any other Secretary of State, became a traveling negotiator, conspicuously the nation's foremost diplomat. So much did he like to travel and negotiate that it was said that to him an airplane was not merely a convenience, it was a temptation.

Dulles started his travels early. Less than ten days after taking office, he jumped over to Europe to persuade our allies to hasten unification for defense. At the end of his six years in office, he had logged some 560,000 miles on affairs of state, more than the distance of a round trip to the moon. He traveled farther, visited more countries, met more statesmen than any other diplomat in history. He considered himself a roving negotiator or trouble shooter, who represented the President's Constitutional authority to conduct foreign relations. He worked out problems directly with foreign statesmen and then left his subordinates to administer his policies in his absence.

"It's silly," Dulles told a television audience after one of his trips abroad, "to go at it the old-fashioned way of exchanging notes, which take a month before you get a good understanding," when by overnight flight and "talking a few minutes face to face," you can do so at once. "I don't think we'll ever go back to the old-fashioned way." After another trip, he spoke of the importance of talking intimately with foreign leaders and asserted that "talking face to face is the best way yet invented for enabling men to understand each other."

There were many, however, who were critical of this approach to the conduct of foreign relations. Since Dulles did all the negotiating himself, critics said, he was reducing ambassadors and other subordinates to mere executors of his policies without diplomatic powers of their own. Others insisted that he should remain at home in full command of the State Department to make decisions when crises arose, particularly since he did not rely on subordinates for aid in the making of policy and appeared to carry the nation's foreign policies in his vest pocket. For a one-man State Department, they insisted, Dulles was traveling too much.

Actually, it was not Dulles alone who had reduced ambassadors to mere symbols, or funnels of information, but also the times—an age that demanded a roving Secretary of State and the technology that made rapid travel possible. Dulles was an agent, not the sole cause, of change in the work of the Secretary.

When Christian Herter, Dulles' successor, took office he told reporters, "I will travel if I feel it is necessary to travel. But as you know I have always been a pretty strong team worker." Yet Herter spent 80 out of his first 115 days away from Washington involved in personal diplomacy.

Kennedy's Secretary, too, announced that he would try to avoid travel, indicating that he believed the Secretary of State should remain at his desk as much as possible. Yet the pressing demands of America's world-wide responsibilities were such that within four months after taking over the Secretaryship, Dean Rusk was away from Washington about as often as he was there, flying to various high-level conferences in Bangkok, Ankara, Oslo, and Geneva.

The use of peripatetic diplomacy is not unique with the Secretary of State. Other foreign ministers, heads of state, and especially the President, have also become globetrotters. The great surge in personal diplomacy and travel on the highest levels has come mainly from the staggering changes in the climate of opinion and the political structure of the world and, for the Secretary, from the vastly expanded responsibilities and world-wide commitments of the United States. Statesmen and peoples all over the world now demand emissaries on the highest levels; they are no longer content to settle important matters through ordinary channels and ambassadors. The extreme sensitiveness of foreign policy to the vagaries of world opinion, to publicity, and to propaganda, seemingly are making the Secretary's globetrotting, and even summit conferences, necessary.

Touching on this theme, a controversial article in *Life* magazine of January, 1956, claimed that Dulles had "altered drastically the basic concept of the job of Secretary of State." He did not, it said, work in the so-called traditional pattern of the administrative executive. He regarded too much time spent in Washington as neglect of American leadership in world affairs, and hence devoted himself fully to personal diplomacy. In contrast to Acheson, Marshall, and Herter, who were team men despite their travels, Dulles seemingly had a romantic view of the Secretaryship, envisioning the Secretary of State as an individual performer on the international stage, a master diplomat who had perfected the art of settling world problems through negotiation.

Actually, Dulles did not fundamentally change the nature of his office. Even though most Secretaries have been politicians and few have had the diplomatic experience he brought to the office, the Secretaryship has always been basically the post of the nation's foremost diplomat. Its link with the diplomacy of the past, in fact, has given it a stability that time and bewildering technological changes have not destroyed. Secretaries such as Jefferson, Monroe, and John Quincy Adams were all skilled diplomats.

Early in the twentieth century, John Hay came as close to being a professional diplomat as anyone who has ever filled the Secretaryship.

Virtually all Secretaries, particularly in the twentieth century, have had to be diplomats regardless of their lack of previous experience, for all have had to meet and negotiate with foreign statesmen, even if they did not travel halfway round the world to do so. Without leaving Washington, Hay, for instance, negotiated the treaties that led to the building of the Panama Canal, Root concluded an important executive agreement with the Japanese, Bryan signed a series of conciliation treaties with foreign governments, and Hughes concluded one naval and two Far Eastern pacts. It can be seen, therefore, that the Secretary of State, regardless of his own deficiencies or the restrictions placed upon him by the President, cannot avoid diplomacy; not even the senile and powerless John Sherman could do so.

II.

In the years of the Cold War, however, the Secretary's diplomacy has received more publicity than ever before, and his own stature has appeared to increase because his power over the shaping of foreign policy seems to grow with the extent of his travels. Actually, the Secretary's relative importance has grown because the President himself can take cognizance of only a small part of the nation's vastly expanded international activities. He is often compelled, therefore, to rely on his Secretary of State and others for help in formulating foreign policy and sometimes for the policy itself.

Seldom, actually, is the Secretary of State alone responsible for abrupt or radical changes in foreign policy. From Secretary to Secretary, Administration to Administration, decade to decade, foreign policy usually manifests a fundamental continuity and a movement so gradual as to seem almost glacial. This is so because foreign policy does not usually spring only from the brain of the Secretary but also emerges from the collaboration of many minds, from time, from experience, and from *ad hoc* situations. In the words of Dean Acheson, "the springs of policy bubble up; they do not trickle down."

It may be convenient to speak of the foreign policy of a Secretary of State, but to do so is frequently misleading, for the day-to-day decisions of the Secretary are often of little consequence in the development of major policies. An idea does not become national policy, as the unthinking believe, merely because the Secretary approves it. The making of foreign policy is one of the highest functions of the state, and in the United States, that power belongs almost exclusively to the President, a power that few Presidents would totally delegate. Most strong Presidents, therefore, tend to deal with major issues and fundamental foreign policy themselves. They usually make the great decisions and leave the lesser ones to their Secretaries of State.

It is frequently this unwillingness of the President to share his power and the desire of the Secretary to grasp power that has led to friction between the Secretaries of State and the Presidents who appointed them. Usually this struggle for power, mainly over the conduct of foreign relations, grows out of a clash of personalities, for, after all, the drive for power is embedded in personality. Only one Secretary was dismissed outright, and this case, that of Timothy Pickering, involved a personality conflict as well as friction over policy and politics. The forced resignations, such as Robert Smith's and Robert Lansing's, also usually hinged on personality conflict.

Out of the fifty-three men who have held the Secretaryship, at least fifteen either quarreled with the President or differed seriously with him over matters of policy. This number excludes those Secretaries who differed with their Presidents in the normal give and take of shaping policy or in the heat of small arguments. In about thirty-five cases, the relations between the President and his Secretary can be described as generally harmonious.

Even though this analysis, admittedly based on limited evidence, may have a disquieting margin of error, the uncomfortable fact remains that the ratio of friction to harmony between the two men who have the major responsibility for the nation's foreign policy has been high. It suggests, too, that the conduct of foreign relations may have suffered at times more from personality conflicts than from technical or professional deficiencies in the Secretary. In fact, only three Secretaries, Jefferson, Pickering, and Bryan, left office over an issue of foreign policy, and Pickering's case turned more on personality.

This analysis also suggests that the intangible factor of personality may at times outweigh a Secretary's intellectual and professional competence in convincing a President that he should share his power over foreign relations with his Secretary of State. A President, like anyone else, is more likely to trust and work comfortably with a man whose personality pleases him than with one whose temperament he finds uncongenial.

Although this conclusion implies that compatible personalities are important in the relationship between a President and his Secretary of State, because that relationship is intensely personal as well as official, it does not indicate that personality should be the decisive factor in the selection of a Secretary. Indeed, Secretaries whose main virtue is that they please the President may do him and their country a disservice, for nothing can substitute for intelligence, professional competence, independent judgment, and ideas in the Secretaryship.

That independence, even though a Secretary acts in the President's name, makes the Secretary of State more than an administrator or a mere figurehead. As a result, despite his reliance on the President and his sometimes humiliating status, the Secretary not infrequently deserves greater credit than anyone else for shaping and carrying out foreign policy. Most Secretaries, in fact, have left an imprint of some kind on the office, on the nation's diplomatic history, and on the foreign policy that has been woven into its diplomatic tradition.

Regardless of the limitations of the Secretaryship, moreover, it can be an office of vast power, one that gives the Secretary a broad opportunity, second only to that in the Presidency itself, to translate his ideas into policy and to play a grand role in world affairs. He, more than any other department head or the Vice-President, has the best chance to attain lasting fame, for he, next to the President, has the largest stage on which to perform. Under a weak, or permissive, President, a bold competent Secretary, one with a strong personality to match sweeping ideas, can achieve a greatness second only to the President and a distinction above that of any other foreign minister.

This, consequently, might lead one to ask by what criteria do we measure effectiveness and accomplishment in a Secretary of State. Although there are more complicated means, for our purpose it seems appropriate to advance the theory that an outstanding Secretary is one who has great ideas and principles, that is ideas that transcend immediate and local problems, one who has been given the power to participate in the making of important decisions and to mold his ideas into policy, and who has the diplomatic skill and statesmanship to carry out that policy in international affairs.

At the same time, the outstanding Secretary is one who retains the over-all direction of foreign policy against the parochial interests of other agencies dealing with foreign affairs. He is one who can establish and maintain his authority within his own department, in the Cabinet, and in his relations with the President. He is one who can keep those with independent political support, from inside his own department and without, from stepping between himself and the President. He is one who realizes that he can refine and enrich decisions, can persuade the President to take action, but does not have to be reminded that he does not himself possess the power of final decision. He is one who is jealous of his prestige and that of his office, for he understands that such prestige is an important tool in carrying out foreign policy.

Finally, the truly great Secretary of State will give style and cohesion to foreign policy as a whole. Even though we have broken down the obligations of the Secretary into categories for purposes of analysis, the outstanding Secretary will always realize also that no one part of his duties, or his office, can be wholly isolated from the other parts, that all belong inseparably to an interacting whole.

The listing of these criteria leads logically to the question: Who are the Secretaries who have come closest to fulfilling them, the Secretaries who stand out above the others? This, in turn, leads to an old game of diplomatic historians and political scientists, that of ranking the Secretaries of State, a game second in popularity only to that of ranking the Presidents. Even though experts are bound to disagree over any listing, we shall nonetheless boldly rank ten of the Secretaries, but not on the usual basis of effectiveness in diplomacy alone. We shall do so only in accordance with the standards in our theory.

Most historians and students of government reserve the first position for John Quincy Adams, and according to our criteria, he deserves it. From his mind sprang the idea of continental expansion, from his diplomacy emerged the Transcontinental Treaty of 1819 that helped make it possible, and from him came the noncolonization principle of the Monroe Doctrine. Moreover, despite great odds, he persuaded President Monroe to make a unilateral pronouncement of the doctrine, and Adams was allowed the power to carry out the policies he advanced. His brilliant accomplishments as Secretary of State are outstanding in a notable public career. He is a great Secretary.

William H. Seward conducted a masterful diplomacy during the Civil War, skillfully helped maneuver the French out of Mexico after Maximilian had established a shaky empire there, almost alone acquired Alaska, and was prominent and powerful in the making of foreign and domestic policy in two crisis-ridden Administrations. He, too, is a great Secretary and merits second place.

Third place goes to Dean Acheson for helping to guide the nation through the perilous and frustrating Korean War, when a diplomatic misstep might have led to a nuclear Armageddon. In his advice to President Truman, he helped to maintain the supremacy of the civil authority over the military leader and courageously refused to allow foreign policy to become secondary to

immediate objectives on the battlefield. His contributions to the
policy of containment and the making of NATO, and his ability
to originate policy and to carry it out despite searing political
criticism, all mark him as a Secretary of unusual ability and
accomplishment.

John Foster Dulles, despite the gusts of controversy that he and
his policies started, originated foreign policy and carried it out.
There is no doubt that he was the dominant figure in the Eisenhower Administrations, a man whose intellectual grasp was
greater than that of his contemporaries in government, a man
who brought the modern Secretaryship virtually to the summit
of its power. He helped conclude the Korean War and despite his
"brinkmanship," or what critics called a reckless flirtation with
war, helped keep the nation at peace in times of crushing crises,
and built up a network of alliances to safeguard the nation. More
than most Secretaries, he showed growth in office and devoted his
life to his work. He fits into fourth place.

Hamilton Fish ranks number five because he, also, was the
leading figure of the Administrations he served. He, too, helped
to keep the nation at peace when war seemed logical, mainly by
diverting President Grant from a determination to free Cuba
from Spain. In addition, he negotiated the monumental Treaty of
Washington. He was the outstanding statesman of his time.

Daniel Webster ranks sixth and Charles E. Hughes seventh
because they clearly commanded foreign relations, were the
sources of ideas in foreign policy, and each was associated with
an outstanding diplomatic accomplishment, the Webster-Ashburton Treaty and the treaties of the Washington Conference of
1921–22.

George C. Marshall takes eighth place for helping to save
Europe from misery and perhaps from Communism with his
Marshall Plan, and John Hay, ninth, for his skilled diplomacy.

Although Henry L. Stimson at times quarreled with President
Hoover over foreign policy and did not have the power in shaping policy that the others on this list had, he was a man of ideas

and gave his office a mark of dignity. As a statesman and thinker, he takes tenth place.

Ironically, this list includes only one of the three Secretaries who won Nobel Peace Prizes. We must remember, however, that those prizes are awarded for special achievement and not for one's power and ideas in the Secretaryship.

Even though every Secretary cannot be outstanding, from the criteria we have used it should be clear that the Secretaryship should not be offered as a political plum and that the Secretary should not be merely a figurehead. Ideally, a man with experience in politics, diplomacy, and administration should hold the office, but under the new urgency of foreign affairs in an age of weapons of unprecedented destructiveness, the specialized ability in international matters, in the art of diplomacy, is more important than the others.

The modern Secretary should, above all, be a statesman and a diplomat in the finest sense, the active head of an organization equipped to act quickly in foreign relations in keeping with the stepped-up tempo of international affairs, a person the President can trust with impressive delegated powers, one so loyal to his chief that he may be allowed to initiate and shape policy. This relationship is essential, for in the American system the making of foreign policy cannot usually be successfully delegated beyond the Secretary of State, and in times of great crisis cannot be delegated at all.

This standard does not mean that the President should abdicate any of his power over foreign affairs or that the Secretary of State must or should take on the full characteristics of a foreign minister, as in the British system. The Secretary can carry on effectively in the traditions of his own unique office, an office whose traditions grow more impressive with each passing year, an office of such dignity that it sheds luster on whoever holds it. This holds true even though a few Secretaries have appeared to have practically no power, for the record of the American Secretary of State compares favorably with that of foreign ministers of virtually any other country.

The Secretaryship, in other words, is flexible enough to be one of the great offices of the world. A President, therefore, should not attempt to be his own Secretary of State, but should use his chosen Secretary to help ease his own immense burden. He should go beyond tradition and assign the Secretary preeminent influence in the government in fact as well as name, especially in the light of the new pressing importance of foreign policy in the nation's welfare. The old boundaries between domestic and foreign policies, we are told, have virtually disappeared. Domestic and defense policies, in fact, are being shaped in large measure by the requirements of foreign policy. Hence, the selection and proper use of the Secretary of State, Americans should realize, is one of the most compelling of their President's duties.

Bibliographical Note

This book rests on a selected use of manuscript sources and a mass of printed works, letters, diaries, memoirs, other personal accounts, biographies, and monographs. Most of the manuscript collections consulted, such as the William McKinley, Whitelaw Reid, John Hay, Theodore Roosevelt, Elihu Root, Philander C. Knox, Woodrow Wilson, William Jennings Bryan, Robert Lansing, and Charles Evans Hughes papers, are in the Manuscript Division of the Library of Congress. I have also used microfilm copies of the Timothy Pickering Papers, in the Massachusetts Historical Society in Boston, material from other collections examined in my earlier researches on the Federalist period, have gone through the Lewis Cass Papers, in the William L. Clements Library of the University of Michigan, have sampled the Herbert Hoover Papers, in the Hoover Library at Stanford University, and have examined a small file of material pertaining to the Secretaryship of State in the Historical Office of the Department of State.

The secondary and printed materials, as well as serials and files of newspapers such as *The New York Times,* may be found in any of a number of good research libraries. The interested specialist should not have difficulty tracing most of my sources from the text, but since this broad study has no formal documentation, the following selected general titles may prove helpful to the reader who may wish to pursue this subject in greater detail.

For almost anyone, the starting point should be Samuel F. Bemis, ed., *The American Secretaries of State and Their Diplomacy* (10 vols., New York: Alfred A. Knopf, 1927-29). This indispensable work covers the individual Secretaries from the beginning of the nation through the Secretaryship of Charles E. Hughes. It has been supplemented, down through the Secretaryship of John Foster Dulles, by Norman A. Graebner, ed., *An Uncertain Tradition: American Secretaries of State in the Twentieth Century* (New York: McGraw-Hill Book Company, 1961), a book of essays by fourteen authors. These essays are valuable because they concentrate more on power, ideas, and key issues in the Secretaryship itself than do the studies in the Bemis series. The only book that offers an analysis of the Secretaryship itself is Don K. Price, ed., *The*

Secretary of State (Englewood Cliffs, N.J.: Prentice-Hall, 1960), another collection of essays. Written by scholars and former government officials, such as Dean Acheson, these essays served as background reading for the Eighteenth American Assembly in 1960. They include more data on the State Department, the making of foreign policy, and other related matters than on the Secretaryship itself. A brief but stimulating analysis of the office is Paul H. Nitze, " 'Impossible' Job of Secretary of State," *The New York Times Magazine*, February 24, 1957, p. 9. E. W. Kenworthy, in "Evolution of Our No. 1 Diplomat," *The New York Times Magazine*, March 18, 1962, p. 31, deals with the Secretaryship of Dean Rusk and stresses that President Kennedy "has learned that he cannot be his own Secretary of State."

Graham H. Stuart, *The Department of State: A History of Its Organization, Procedure, and Personnel* (New York: The Macmillan Company, 1949), briefly describes the main contribution of each Secretary to foreign policy and to the history of the State Department but is most useful for information on the administrative responsibilities of the Secretaries. The most recent analysis of the department and its administration, Robert E. Elder, *The Policy Machine: The Department of State and American Foreign Policy* (Syracuse, N.Y.: Syracuse University Press, 1960), concentrates on policy-making procedures. Another recent study, Henry Field Haviland, Jr., *et al., The Formulation and Administration of United States Foreign Policy* (Washington, D.C.: Brookings Institution, 1960), deals with various agencies, besides the State Department, involved in the making of foreign policy. It urges, among other proposals, the creation of a super Secretary of State, "a secretary in the sense that Washington regarded Jefferson or Hamilton." An older but still valuable study of the State Department, which, like the Stuart history, also stresses administration is Gaillard Hunt, *The Department of State of the United States: Its History and Functions* (New Haven, Conn.: Yale University Press, 1914). For an analysis of the British equivalent of the State Department, see William Strang *et al., The Foreign Office* (London: Allen & Unwin, 1955) and Donald G. Bishop, *The Administration of British Foreign Relations* (Syracuse, N.Y.: Syracuse University Press, 1961). For diplomatic practice, see Graham H. Stuart, *American Diplomatic and Consular Practice* (2d ed.; New York: Appleton-Century-Crofts, 1952); Warren F. Ilchman, *Professional Diplomacy in the United States, 1779–1939: A Study in Administrative History* (Chicago: The University of Chicago Press, 1961); Charles W. Thayer, *Diplomat* (New York: Harper & Brothers, 1959); and Katherine Crane, *Mr. Carr of State: Forty-Seven Years in the Department of State* (New York: St Martin's Press, 1960). Power as a political concept, and the shaping and sharing of power, are analyzed in Harold D. Lasswell and Abraham Kaplan, *Power and Society: A Framework for Political Inquiry* (New Haven, Conn.: Yale University Press, 1950). The standard work on the American Cabinet system is Henry B.

Learned, *The President's Cabinet: Studies in the Origin, Formation and Structure of An American Institution* (New Haven, Conn.: Yale University Press, 1912). See also Mary L. Hinsdale, *A History of the President's Cabinet* (Ann Arbor, Mich.: George Wahr Publishing Company, 1911), and for the later period, Richard F. Fenno, Jr., *The President's Cabinet: An Analysis in the Period from Wilson to Eisenhower* (Cambridge, Mass.: Harvard University Press, 1959). Stephen Horn, *The Cabinet and Congress* (New York: Columbia University Press, 1960), concentrates on the relationship between the legislative and executive power in the government.

There are a number of books on the Presidency that may be consulted with profit. Edward S. Corwin, *The President, Office and Powers, 1787–1957: History and Analysis of Practice and Opinion* (4th rev. ed.; New York: New York University Press, 1957), has long been the standard work in the field and is especially strong on Constitutional questions. A unique study of personal power, that is, of the President's problem of obtaining power for himself, of keeping it, and of using it, is Richard E. Neustadt, *Presidential Power: The Politics of Leadership* (New York: John Wiley and Sons, 1960). Sidney Hyman, *The American President* (New York: Harper & Brothers, 1954), is a readable and perceptive popular analysis; Harold J. Laski, *The American Presidency: An Interpretation* (New York: Harper & Brothers, 1940), is well written and provocative. Dean Rusk, in "The President," *Foreign Affairs,* XXXVIII (April, 1960), 353–69, discusses the problem of summit diplomacy and the Presidency. Also useful are Clinton Rossiter, *The American Presidency* (New York: Harcourt, Brace and Company, 1956) and Wilfred E. Binkley, *The Man in the White House: His Powers and Duties* (Baltimore: The Johns Hopkins Press, 1959). For an account of the President's unofficial advisers and biographical studies of several, such as Edward House and Harry Hopkins, see Louis W. Koenig, *The Invisible Presidency* (New York: Holt, Rinehart and Winston, 1960).

For a detailed history that places the Secretaryship in the broad context of administrative problems within the Federal Government, see Leonard D. White's study, which earned him a Pulitzer Prize, *The Federalists: A Study in Administrative History* (New York: The Macmillan Company, 1948); *The Jeffersonians: A Study in Administrative History, 1801–1829* (New York: The Macmillan Company, 1951); *The Jacksonians: A Study in Administrative History, 1829–1861* (New York: The Macmillan Company, 1954); *The Republican Era, 1869–1901: A Study in Administrative History* (New York: The Macmillan Company, 1958).

Although there are many biographies of individual Secretaries of State, three of them, all of which won their authors the Pulitzer Prize, stand out: Samuel F. Bemis, *John Quincy Adams and the Foundations of American Foreign Policy* (New York: Alfred A. Knopf, 1949); Allan Nevins, *Hamilton Fish: The Inner History of the Grant Administration*

(New York: Dodd, Mead and Company, 1936); and Tyler Dennett, *John Hay: From Poetry to Politics* (New York: Dodd, Mead and Company, 1933). Another prize-winning study that throws light on the Secretaryship from the point of view of a personal adviser to the President is Robert E. Sherwood, *Roosevelt and Hopkins: An Intimate History* (New York: Harper & Brothers, 1948).

For insights on the Secretaryship in later years as recorded by insiders, the following memoirs are among the most useful: Henry L. Stimson and McGeorge Bundy, *On Active Service in Peace and War* (New York: Harper & Brothers, 1948); *The Memoirs of Cordell Hull* (2 vols., New York: The Macmillan Company, 1948); *Memoirs by Harry S. Truman* (2 vols., Garden City, N. Y.: Doubleday & Company, 1955–56); and Sherman Adams, *Firsthand Report: The Story of the Eisenhower Administration* (New York: Harper & Brothers, 1961).

Index

Acheson, Dean G.: 32, 40, 141, 164; accomplishments, 162, 171–72; as administrator, 159; appointment, 47; attacks against, 144–45; 147; on George Marshall, 18; on policymaking, 168; power of, 121–22; on President, 24; ranking of, 171–72; on Secretaryship, 154

Adams, Henry: on Hay, 96; on Sherman's appointment, 52; on Secretaryship, 137

Adams, John: 10, 60, 65, 66; feud with Pickering, 33, 37, 44, 127; and John Marshall, 112; on Secretaryship, 39, 40

Adams, John Quincy: 41, 137; accomplishments, 37–38, 161; as administrator, 155; appointment, 56; as diplomat, 162, 166; and Henry Clay, 49–50; power of, 115; on Presidential relationship, 114; on Presidential succession, 65, 67; qualifications, 57; ranking of, 171; on Secretaryship, 134–35

Adee, Alvey A., 157

Alaska: acquisition of, 161, 162, 171

Appleton, John, 92

Arthur, Chester A., 59

Articles of Confederation, 3, 11

Atlantic Conference (1941), 25, 105

Babcock, Orville, 27

Bacon, Robert, 45

Barlow, Joel, 127

Bayard, Thomas F., 58, 116

Black, Jeremiah S.: appointment, 45; political adviser, 34; power of, 74

Blaine, James G.: 161; appointment, 59, 71; power of, 24, 79–81, 93; on Secretaryship, 112

Blaine, Mrs. James G.: on Harrison, 93, 94; on Secretaryship, 19, 80

Bowles, Chester, 64

British Guiana–Venezuela boundary dispute (1895), 117, 161

Bryan, William Jennings: 28, 156; appointment, 53–54; as diplomat, 167; influence, 142–43; power of, 98–99; resignation, 128–29, 169

Buchanan, James: 34; appointment, 58, 69; and Black, 45, 74; on Cass, 92–93; power of, 89–91, 128; on Presidential succession, 69–70; on Secretaryship, 90, 91

Bullitt, William C., 104

Burleson, Albert, 100

Burr, Aaron, 65

Byrnes, James F.: 59, 131, 164; on administration, 158–59; appointment, 62–63; power of, 83–84; relations with Truman, 125–26; on Secretaryship, 32, 148–49

Cabinet: 49, 67; under Buchanan, 74; Jackson's use of, 88; nature of, 31–32; under F. D. Roosevelt, 108–9; Secretary of State in, 23

Cairo Conference (1943), 106

Calhoun, John C.: appointment, 58; power of, 73; Presidential relationship, 123; on Secretaryship, 38

Carr, Wilbur J., 157

Casablanca Conference (1943), 106

Cass, Lewis: appointment, 58–59, 91; power of, 92–93; resignation, 128

Churchill, Winston, 25, 105–6

Clay, Henry: 69, 137; as administrator, 155; appointment, 49–50, 67–68; on J. Q. Adams, 57

Clayton, John M.: 58, 73–74; 150

Cleveland, Grover: on Bayard, 116; on Gresham, 61; on Olney, 45, 117; relationship with Secretaries of State, 116

Colby, Bainbridge, 21, 45

Commission on Organization of the Executive Branch. See Hoover Commission

Committee for Foreign Affairs, 2, 4

Congress: 136–37; and executive departments (1779), 4; and foreign affairs (1782), 7–8; ratification of treaties by, 137; and Secretary for Foreign Affairs, 4, 9; and Secretary of State, 23, 137, 140–41, 148

Coolidge, Calvin, 59, 152; on Hughes, 83; and Kellogg, 46, 120

Cuba, 110, 172

Day, William R.: as administrator, 158; appointment, 45; power of, 95
De Gaulle, Charles, 105
Department of Foreign Affairs (1781), 4–5; (1789), 14
Department of State: administration of, 154–55; allegations of Communist infiltration (1950), 146; Constitutional provision for, 12; created, 14–15; distrusted by F. D. Roosevelt, 20, 108
Department of the Treasury, 15
Dewey, Thomas E., 48
Diplomacy: 162; peripatetic, 163–64, 166; Secretary's role in, 166–67
Disarmament conferences: London (1930), 163; Washington (1921–22), 161–62
Dollar Diplomacy, 161
Dulles, John Foster: 19, 35, 41, 48, 85, 126, 164–65; accomplishments, 162; as administrator, 160; attacks against, 147–48; and Congressional committees, 140; and duties of Secretary of State, 21–23; power of, 35–36; 84–86; and press, 36–37, 149–50, 166; ranking of, 172

Eden, Anthony, 106–7
Eisenhower, Dwight D.: 35; and Dulles, 35–36, 48, 84, 86, 148; popularity of, 150; prestige of, 126
European Recovery Program. *See* Marshall Plan
Evarts, William L.: 34; as administrator, 155–56; appointment, 60; power of, 115–16
Everett, Edward, 58
Executive departments: establishment of, 12, 13, 14–15

Fillmore, Millard, 59, 73
Fish, Hamilton: 156; accomplishments, 161; and Grant, 35; power of, 35, 78–79; ranking of, 172; on unofficial advisers, 27
Florida: acquisition of, 162
Foreign policy: continuity of, 167–68. *See also* President
Forsyth, John: as administrator, 154; appointment, 58
Foster, John W., 41, 48, 158
Four-Nation Declaration (1943), 163
Four-Power Treaty (1921), 82–83
Fourteen Points (1918), 101
Franklin, Benjamin, 1, 2, 3, 37
Frelinghuysen, Frederick T., 58, 158

Gallatin, Albert, 55–56
Gardoqui, Diego de, 10–11
Garfield, James A., 71
Grant, Ulysses S.: 60; and Fish, 35, 79; and unofficial advisers, 27
Gresham, Walter Q.: appointment, 61; power of, 116–17
Grey, Sir Edward, 98

Hamilton, Alexander: 3, 11; and foreign policy, 19–20, 24, 32, 42
Hanna, Mark, 51–52
Harding, Warren G.: 35, 61; on Hughes, 82; on Japanese treaty, 83
Harding, Mrs. Warren G., 82
Harriman, W. Averell, 107
Harrison, Benjamin: appointment of Blaine, 59; control of foreign policy, 80, 93–94
Harrison, William Henry, 69, 72
Hawaii: annexation of, 95
Hay, John: 19; accomplishments, 161; on administration, 157; appointment, 45; on Congress, 136, 137, 151–52; as diplomat, 41, 167; on duties of Secretary, 135; and politics, 136, 142; power under McKinley, 118–19; power under T. Roosevelt, 96–97; ranking of, 172
Hayes, Rutherford B.: 34, 60; and Evarts, 116
Herter, Christian A.: 160–61, 165; appointment, 41; popularity of, 150; training, 47
Hitler, Adolf, 104
Hobart, Garret A., 19
Hoover, Herbert: on Hughes and Harding, 83; on politics, 142; and Stimson, 61, 124–25, 142
Hoover Commission, 152–53, 160
Hoover Doctrine. *See* Stimson Doctrine
Hopkins, Harry: and Hull, 143; and Lend-Lease, 107–8; power of, 29–30
House, Edward M.: on Lansing, 29, 99–100, 101; power of, 28-29
Hughes, Charles Evans: 35, 46; accomplishments, 161–62; as administrator, 158; appointment, 61; as diplomat, 167; power of, 81–83; ranking of, 172
Hull, Cordell: accomplishments, 162, 163; as administrator, 158; appointment, 61–62, 103; Gallup poll on, 71, 109; humiliated, 24–25; political influence, 141, 143–44; power of, 20, 24–26, 30–31, 103, 141; Presidential aspirant, 71; on relation-

ship with President, 108–9; on Secretaryship, 17, 109; on Sumner Welles, 25, 104
Hunter, William, 157

Ickes, Harold L., 26, 147

Jackson, Andrew: 34; opposition to Presidential aspirants, 68; and political qualifications of Secretary, 57; use of Secretary, 88
Jay, John: accomplishments, 11–12; on committee system, 3; distrusted by Congress, 11; as Secretary for Foreign Affairs, 8; French evaluation of, 10; on power, 9, 10–11; treaty with England (1794), 162
Jefferson, Thomas: 24, 37, 55, 65, 151, 162; clash with Hamilton, 42; diplomat, 166; first Secretary of State, 17; on Madison, 114; on Monroe and J. Q. Adams, 115; on President, 87; on Secretaryship, 133
Johnson, Andrew, 34, 59, 78, 142

Kellogg, Frank B.: accomplishments, 162, 163; as administrator, 158; appointment, 46; power of, 120
Kellogg-Briand Antiwar Pact, 162
Kennedy, John F.: 63; control of foreign policy, 110; on Congress and the Secretary, 23
Knox, Philander C.: accomplishments, 161; as administrator, 156–57; power of, 34, 81
Korean War, 122, 162, 171, 172

Lansing, Robert: 48; appointment, 28–29, 46; on Bryan, 143; on House, 29; power of, 99–102; resignation, 33–34, 129–30, 168; on Wilson, 101, 102
League of Nations, 101, 143
Leahy, William D., 105
Lee, Arthur, 5
Lend-Lease Administration, 107
Lincoln, Abraham: appointment of Seward, 50–51; reliance on Seward, 31, 75–76
Lincoln, Mrs. Abraham, 77
Livingston, Edward: appointment, 57; on Secretaryship, 18
Livingston, Robert R.: evaluated, 7; on power, 6; on Secretaryship for Foreign Affairs, 5
Louisiana Purchase, 162
Lovell, James, 2–3
Lusitania notes (1915), 98–99

McAdoo, William G., 100
McCarthy, Joseph R., 146, 149
McKinley, William: 45, 51; assassination, 19; control of foreign policy, 95; rejects Hay's resignation, 118–19, 152; on Sherman, 52–53
McLane, Louis: as administrator, 154–55; appointment, 57–58
Madison, James: 7, 12, 65; appointment, 55; power of, 113–14; on removal power, 13; on Secretaryship, 133–34; on Secretaryship of Foreign Affairs, 9; and Robert Smith, 88, 127
Marcy, William L., 58, 92
Marshall, George C.: 18, 21, 41, 47, 164; accomplishments, 162; as administrator, 159; appointment, 44; power of, 120–21; and Presidential succession, 71–72; ranking of, 172
Marshall, John: on loyalty, 44; power of, 112–13
Marshall Plan, 121, 162, 172
Moley, Raymond, 24
Monroe, James: 65, 171; on J. Q. Adams, 57; appointment, 56; control of foreign policy, 114–15; as diplomat, 41, 166; on Secretaryship, 31, 133, 134
Monroe Doctrine, 161, 171
Montevideo Conference (1933), 163
Morgenthau, Henry, Jr., 26, 106
Morris, Gouverneur, 2
Moscow Conference (1945), 125
Mussolini, Benito, 104–5

National Security Council, 23
NATO, 162, 172
Nixon, Richard M., 19
Nonrecognition doctrine. *See* Stimson Doctrine

Olney, Richard: accomplishments, 161; appointment, 45; power of, 117
Onís, Luis de, 38, 162
Open Door Policy, 161
Oregon: acquisition of, 38
Oumansky, Constantin, 105

Paine, Thomas, 2
Panama Canal, 167
Peace Conference (1919), 101, 163
Pickering, Timothy: 33, 44, 128, 168; on Secretaryship, 44
Policy Planning Staff, 159, 160
Politics, 23–24, 41, 57, 132–33, 141–42

Polk, James K.: appointment, 58; control of foreign policy, 89–90; on Buchanan, 70, 89, 155; opposition to Presidential aspirants, 69
Potsdam Conference (1945), 164
Power in Secretaryship, 38, 77–79, 110–11, 168–70
President: consultation with Secretary, 24, 30–31; his own Secretary, 97, 100, 110, 111, 174; power over foreign policy, 16, 87, 138, 167–68; power over Secretary for the Department of Foreign Affairs, 14; and second Secretary of State, 44–47; and succession of Secretary, 19, 62–63, 65–66, 72; unofficial advisers to, 26, 88–89

Randolph, Edmund: quarrel with Washington, 18, 43, 127; resignation, 43, 151
Reciprocal Trade Agreements Program (1934), 162
Rogers Act (1924), 158
Roosevelt, Franklin D.: distrust of State Department, 20, 108; political value of Secretary, 61–62, 143; and Presidential succession, 71; and unofficial advisers, 24–26
Roosevelt, Theodore: 59, 71; on Bacon, 45; and Congress, 138; on Hay, 97, 136, 142; on power of Secretary, 37; and Presidential succession, 19; on Root, 37, 119
Root, Elihu: as administrator, 157–58; appointment, 45, 71; and Congress, 138; as diplomat, 167; power of, 37, 119
Rusk, Dean: 165–66; appointment, 63–64; power of, 110

SEATO, 162
Secretary for Foreign Affairs: 4–5, 6, 10; title changed, 6
Senate Committee on Foreign Relations, 138, 139
Seward, William H.: accomplishments, 161, 162; appointment, 50–51; influence, 142, 151; power of, 31, 34, 74–78; ranking of, 171
Sherman, John: 167; appointment, 51–53; resignation, 95; on Secretaryship, 53
Smith, Robert: attack on Madison, 127; appointment, 56; power of, 88; resignation, 168
Smith, Samuel, 56
Soviet Union, 104

Stettinius, Edward R., Jr.: 59, 63, 163; as administrator, 155, 158; appointment, 46–47, 109–10
Stevenson, Adlai E., 63–64
Stimson, Henry L.: accomplishments, 162, 163; appointment, 61; ranking of, 172–73; and Hoover, 21, 124; on Secretaryship, 132, 142
Stimson Doctrine, 124–25, 162
Suez crisis (1956), 148

Taft, Robert A., 48
Taft, William H., 34, 81
Taylor, Zachary, 73, 150
Teheran Conference (1944), 106
Texas: annexation of, 73, 123–24
Thomson, Charles, 1, 8
Transcontinental Treaty (1819), 161, 171
Truman, Harry S.: 41–42, 59, 171; on Acheson, 32–33, 47, 122, 123, 147; on George Marshall, 120, 121; and Byrnes, 62, 63, 84, 125, 126, 130–31; on Secretaryship, 18, 20, 120; use of Cabinet, 32
Tumulty, Joseph, 129, 130
Tyler, John, 35, 58, 73

Van Buren, Martin: 34, 60; appointment, 57, 68; power of, 89; resignation, 69
Venezuela–British Guiana boundary dispute (1895), 117, 161

Wallace, Henry A., 25–26, 32
Washburne, Elihu B., 60
Washington, George: and origins of Cabinet, 31–32; and political appointments, 42; and Randolph, 18, 43, 127; on Secretaryship, 18
Washington, Treaty of (1871), 161, 172
Webster, Daniel: 35, 58; accomplishments, 161; appointment, 59, 69; power of, 72–73; ranking of, 172
Webster-Ashburton Treaty, 161, 172
Weed, Thurlow, 144
Welles, Gideon, 77
Welles, Sumner: and Hull, 104, 143–44; influence of, 25
Wilson, Woodrow: 28, 45; and Bryan, 53, 54–55, 98–99, 128–29, 142–43; control of foreign policy, 98, 100; and Lansing, 33–34, 99–103, 129–30
World Economic Conference (1933), 24, 104, 163

Yalta Conference (1945), 110